THE
EVERYTHING.
LUCID DREAMING
BOOK

Dear Reader,

The idea of writing a book on lucid dreaming was very intriguing to me. Being in the metaphysical field for over twenty years and having written books about psychic development, I was already familiar with the important role that dreams and dream interpretation play in our lives, whether we know it or not. As a specialist in hypnosis and neuro-linguistic programming (NLP), I have been inducing trance-like dream states in people ever since I started my practice; lucid dreaming employs many of the same concepts that I use in inducing hypnotic or altered states of consciousness trances.

My fascination with how minds work started many years ago when I became aware that I just did not think the way others did. Most of my life has been a struggle, trying to pretend that I knew what other people know. NLP taught me that I am different, and so are you. We all are. I am nonvisual, which means that I have no pictures in my mind's eye. I don't even dream as most people do, and yet dreams are an important part of the way I am guided through life. May this book help bring you guidance in your life.

Michael R. Hathaway

Welcome to the EVERYTHING® Series!

These handy, accessible books give you all you need to tackle a difficult project, gain a new hobby, comprehend a fascinating topic, prepare for an exam, or even brush up on something you learned back in school but have since forgotten.

You can choose to read an Everything® book from cover to cover or just pick out the information you want from our four useful boxes: e-questions, e-facts, e-alerts, and e-ssentials.

We give you everything you need to know on the subject, but throw in a lot of fun stuff along the way, too.

We now have more than 400 Everything® books in print, spanning such wide-ranging categories as weddings, pregnancy, cooking, music instruction, foreign language, crafts, pets, New Age, and so much more. When you're done reading them all, you can finally say you know Everything®!

QUESTION

Answers to common questions

FACT

Important snippets of information

ALERT

Urgent warnings

ESSENTIAL

Quick handy tips

PUBLISHER Karen Cooper

DIRECTOR OF ACQUISITIONS AND INNOVATION Paula Munier

MANAGING EDITOR, EVERYTHING® SERIES Lisa Laing

COPY CHIEF Casey Ebert

ASSISTANT PRODUCTION EDITOR Melanie Cordova

ACQUISITIONS EDITOR Lisa Laing

ASSOCIATE DEVELOPMENT EDITOR Hillary Thompson

EDITORIAL ASSISTANT Ross Weisman

EVERYTHING® SERIES COVER DESIGNER Erin Alexander

LAYOUT DESIGNERS Erin Dawson, Michelle Roy Kelly, Elisabeth Lariviere, Denise Wallace

Visit the entire Everything® series at *www.everything.com*

THE
EVERYTHING®
LUCID DREAMING BOOK

Use your dreams to solve problems, improve
creativity, and understand yourself

Michael R. Hathaway, DCH

Adamsmedia
Avon, Massachusetts

This book is dedicated to my family
and friends, as well as all the dreamers
of the world who seek answers
beyond normal conscious reality.

An Everything® Series Book.
Everything® and everything.com® are registered trademarks of F+W Media, Inc.

Published by Adams Media, a division of F+W Media, Inc.
57 Littlefield Street, Avon, MA 02322 U.S.A.
www.adamsmedia.com

ISBN 10: 1-4405-2855-1
ISBN 13: 978-1-4405-2855-2
eISBN 10: 1-4405-3133-1
eISBN 13: 978-1-4405-3133-0

Printed in the United States of America.

10 9 8 7 6 5 4 3 2 1

Library of Congress Cataloging-in-Publication Data
is available from the publisher.

This publication is designed to provide accurate and authoritative information with regard to the subject matter covered. It is sold with the understanding that the publisher is not engaged in rendering legal, accounting, or other professional advice. If legal advice or other expert assistance is required, the services of a competent professional person should be sought.

—From a *Declaration of Principles* jointly adopted by a Committee of the American Bar Association and a Committee of Publishers and Associations

Many of the designations used by manufacturers and sellers to distinguish their products are claimed as trademarks. Where those designations appear in this book and Adams Media was aware of a trademark claim, the designations have been printed with initial capital letters.

This book is available at quantity discounts for bulk purchases.
For information, please call 1-800-289-0963.

Contents

Acknowledgments

I would like to thank the pioneers in the field of lucid dreaming, such as Celia Green and Stephen LaBerge, for helping to create techniques that have helped countless people to better their lives. Also, thanks to C. Scott Moss for his work on hypnotic dream investigations, and for guidance from Dr. Lisa Halpin, and especially to the expert editing of my wife, Penny.

The Top 10 Reasons to Try Lucid Dreaming

1. Lucid dreaming can help create positive changes in your life.

2. You can use your mind's eye to create lucid dream intentions that will amplify your lucid dreaming experience.

3. You can change your nightmares through lucid dreaming.

4. Lucid dreaming gives you the power to take control of your dreams.

5. You can identify and develop your psychic abilities through your lucid dreams.

6. Lucid dreaming can help you deepen your faith.

7. Lucid dreaming can connect you with your angels and spirit guides.

8. You can examine your fears through your lucid dreams.

9. Lucid dreaming can help you hone your athletic skills or develop an artistic talent.

10. Lucid dreaming provides a tool to look at life situations with the freedom to consider solutions from many different views.

Introduction

THIS IS NOT JUST another book about dreaming. It shows you in a simple and enjoyable way how to combine the techniques of working with and controlling your nightly dreams and how to identify and use your natural ability to imagine in your mind's eye. Most people dream. Many have learned or are interested in learning how to understand their dreams. This book goes a step further and shows you how to consciously work with and manipulate your dreams as well as how to create dream trances.

Unless you are familiar with the process of lucid dreaming, you may have a misconception about what it really is. Lucid dreaming is a natural experience that most people have had sometime in their lives. You may have become aware that you were flying through the air as free as a bird, propelled by some sort of energy that you could control. You may have found yourself involved in the dream and consciously directing the role you were playing. If you have had an experience like this, you were actually lucid dreaming.

The same misconceptions about lucid dreaming often apply to hypnosis. Hypnosis is also a natural phenomenon experienced daily by almost everyone. Simply explained, hypnosis is an altered state of consciousness that can be experienced on many levels of awareness, ranging from a light daydream to a powerful hallucination where the person has lost touch with what is actually happening around him. In this book, you will come to understand the connection between lucid dreaming and hypnotic trances, identified here as altered states of consciousness lucid-dream trances. You will learn how you constantly enter into your natural trances and how to create positive mental images that can help you achieve your life goals.

The same year that C. Scott Moss's book *The Hypnotic Investigation of Dreams* was published (1967), Stephen LaBerge began to research lucid dreaming, an ability he discovered he had during his early teenage years. Through his doctoral work on the subject at Stanford University, he developed new techniques to help teach how to induce and consciously manipulate lucid dreams for a variety of purposes. Moss's book concludes that "hypnotically induced and spontaneous dreams, is in the final analysis, correctly viewed as only one aspect of a still broader issue that pervades the whole field of hypnosis studies."

You will learn several techniques to help you induce and experience lucid dreams and lucid dream trances. They include how to consciously intend that you will have a dream in the night, how to enter back into a dream after you have woken up from one, and how to create dream trances anytime you want. It makes no difference whether you are a proficient lucid dreamer or not. You can use lucid dream trances to help you achieve similar results.

This book is easy and nontechnical, and you may be amazed at what you are going to discover about yourself. In fact, it may open the door to some incredible dream adventures, for fun, for self-improvement, or for spiritual guidance. If you have not yet experienced the world of lucid dreaming, this book may just open the door that can change your life for the better. Enjoy, and sweet dreams.

CHAPTER 1

What Are Lucid Dreams?

In this chapter, you will begin to consider the world of lucid dreaming, what it is and how it differs from regular dreams. You will see that there are many benefits to lucid dreaming and very little potential danger. You will learn about the four stages of sleep that you re-experience several times over the course of a night, and what REM is and how it relates to lucid dreaming.

An Overview of Lucid Dreaming

You may already be an experienced lucid dream journeyer, but you may never have considered the topic before. Something must have peaked your interest to cause you to pick up this book. No matter what your level of knowledge or experience on the subject, the goal is to help you better understand the world of lucid dreaming on a level that is right for you. In fact, you have probably experienced at least one lucid dream sometime during your life.

FACT

In his book *Conscious Dreaming,* Robert Moss prefers to use the term "conscious dreaming" rather than "lucid dreaming." The goals of this book are to offer different views and ways for you to develop a style of lucid dreaming that suits your purpose and becomes a useful tool for you to use throughout your life.

The word "lucid," when connected to the mind, refers to being consciously aware of one's thoughts, while the word "dream," to most of us, is the sensory-image experience we have when we are in sleep mode. At first thought, the two words linked together almost contradict each other—being aware while you are in a dream. One possible definition of a lucid dream is that you are consciously aware of what is going on in your dream that is created in your unconscious mind.

Conscious and Unconscious Minds

This book refers to having two different minds, your conscious mind and your unconscious mind (also referred to by other sources as your subconscious mind). Your conscious mind is focused on whatever you are thinking or doing at a particular moment. It is constantly receiving information and making decisions. It is the intellectual or thinking part of your mind. When your conscious mind is engaged, you are aware of what is taking place around you, and you are constantly involved by evaluating what you are focused on.

Your unconscious mind is the storage facility for all of your memories at this point in your life. It is constantly taking in information, much of which you are not consciously aware of. When you dream, your unconscious mind often uses information it has stored to help create the images in your dream experience. Normally, when the unconscious mind takes over, the conscious mind suspends its critical thinking. It isn't until the images in the unconscious mind have faded that the conscious mind becomes aware again.

In a lucid dream, the conscious mind is actually aware of the images being created by the unconscious mind. As a result, the conscious mind has the opportunity to control the images coming from the unconscious mind. When the dreamer realizes this, she now has the opportunity to control her dream. In a regular nonlucid dream, the dream is not in control of the dreamer.

Lucid Dream States

Most people think of lucid dreaming as waking up sometime during the night or other sleep periods and becoming aware that they are still dreaming. That is not the only way that lucid dreaming can be accomplished. You can also enter a lucid dream from a waking state. The dreamer begins by inducing a trance state, such as self-hypnosis, that opens the connection to the unconscious mind and its reality. The conscious mind is still aware enough to interact with the images that the unconscious mind is creating.

ESSENTIAL

The concept of lucid or conscious dreaming is thousands of years old. It can be a magical experience for anyone who wants to try it. You can train yourself to use various lucid dreaming techniques while you are sleeping, after you have woken up from a dream, and through the use of altered states of consciousness.

Out-of-body experiences, shamanic journeys, and other trance experiences are also associated with conscious or lucid dreaming. Near-death experiences are often experienced consciously, even though the spirit has entered some sort of a nonearthly plane. There seems to be an expansion of consciousness that occurs for the participant during a lucid or conscious dream as well as in a mystical experience.

Lucid Dreams Versus Regular Dreams

The question is, how do you know when you are having a lucid dream rather than a regular dream? The difference is that in a lucid dream, you are consciously aware that you are having a dream. Once you become consciously aware, you are free to examine what you are dreaming while you are dreaming it.

Regardless of how vivid the dream was when you were having it, if it ended when you woke up or it stopped when you became consciously aware of it, it was not a lucid dream. For the dream to qualify as a lucid dream, you need to be consciously aware that you are dreaming. Two processes must be taking place at the same time; one is the dream, and the other is conscious thought or awareness. As this book progresses, you will be taught how to prove to yourself that you are consciously aware that you are dreaming.

ALERT

Some people go so far as to act out their dream experiences through sleepwalking or crying out loud. Some might even talk in a foreign language. Through hypnosis, it was found that a subject could actually travel during sleep, but they are not lucid dreams unless the dreamer is consciously aware of what she is doing at the time.

Lucid or conscious dreams can be just as full of symbols as a regular dream. So can dreams of the past and dreams of the future. Psychic dreams, past-life dreams, and healing dreams can all play out as lucid or nonlucid dreams. It all boils down to whether or not the conscious mind is aware when the dream is taking place.

Deep Dreaming

You may wake up abruptly from a vivid dream, such as a nightmare, and not be able to tell for a moment whether it was real or not. You may feel disorientated or nearly overcome by the emotions of the dream. Your heart may be racing, or you may have had a pleasurable experience that you would like to hold onto. All the details of the dream are still clear in your mind's eye. Later on, you will learn how to get back into a dream and turn it into a lucid dream.

FACT

In hypnosis, a person capable of entering into a deep trance state is known as a somnambulant subject. On average, only between 10 and 20 percent of all subjects are considered able to meet the criteria for this deep trance state. The subjects in the 10–20 percentiles usually have a strong imagination.

On the other side of the coin, it is possible to enter such a deep trance from a waking state of consciousness that contact with the conscious mind is lost. In this condition, the subject is not only unaware of what is being experienced during the trance or altered state, he may not have any remembrance after he regains consciousness.

A favorite hypnosis stage show trick is to suggest to a subject while in a deep trance that he will not remember anything that he has done while under hypnosis. He is then brought out of the trance, and, to the amusement of the audience, is unable to remember. When the hypnotist takes away the suggestion, the subject is "shocked" to learn what he has been doing while in the trance.

Benefits of Lucid Dreaming

So, are there any benefits to lucid or conscious dreaming? That is the question often asked by those who have not experienced it. The answer would be that this process is a natural part of the sleep and dream world, and those who recognize it generally agree that there are many benefits to lucid dreaming. In fact, the dreamer is only limited by the boundaries that he sets in his conscious mind.

Lucid dreaming provides you with a technique that lets you control the reality in the dream and gives you the power to change the dream in any way you want. Imagine that you could experience what it was like to actually fly without the need for a plane, and to do so in total control. You could choose how high or how fast or even where you want to go. You are the captain of your journey. Many people begin their lucid dreaming with flying experiences. Lucid dreamers can consciously work through and change a nightmare that has plagued them during regular dreams. They can consciously change the outcome or examine the nightmare from a different perspective. They have the opportunity to confront their fears as they consciously manipulate themselves through the dream. The experience can be empowering for the dreamer in many aspects of his life, knowing that he is in charge of his destiny.

What do you want lucid dreams to do for you?

- **Provide answers to your problems.** You have the chance to dream various outcomes and weigh the results to determine what produces the best solutions for problems you may have been struggling with. You can look at situations without getting caught up in the emotions that may be connected to them during your normal waking state. Imagine what it would be like to get up in the morning with the solution in mind.
- **Help develop your creative talents.** You can practice a musical instrument or rehearse a dance step or enjoy the thrill of a flawless performance in front of adoring fans. You can feel yourself improving night after night as you gain confidence in your abilities. You can even try out a recipe that you create while lucid dreaming.
- **Improve your athletic skills.** You can hone your golf swing or shoot baskets and develop muscle memory to help you repeat your positive lucid dream experiences during an actual athletic event. Remember that you are the captain of your lucid dreams.
- **Help build your confidence.** Would you like to overcome stage fright? You can practice giving great talks or comedy acts, all delivered without a hitch. Hone your skills in front of appreciative audiences that hang on your every word. You can play a leading role with any star you choose during a lucid dream.
- **Work on health issues.** You can work on your weight or any habit that you want to change. You can relieve stress or help a doctor treat a medical situation. You can consult with the best medical minds that are available to you in your lucid dreams.

- **Travel.** You can go on vacation every night to any destination you desire once you have mastered the technique of lucid dreaming. You can take a trip to visit a friend or journey to an exotic location in lush tropic surroundings. You can even travel back in time to visit history if that is your desire, or even into the future.
- **Create a fantasy.** Pure fantasy and pleasure is another motivation for experiencing a lucid dream. It is possible to wake in the middle of a sexual fantasy and be fully aware and able to experience the pleasure as the dream plays out in your conscious mind. You might also choose to determine the dream's outcome.

You can travel into the spiritual realms of the universe through your lucid dreams and consult with your spirit guides or the angels that watch over you. You can travel to the Akashic Records, where the memories of your soul are kept. You can consult with the brilliant minds that have shaped the history of the past. You can journey to the core of the universe. Remember that the benefits of lucid dreaming are limitless.

Is Lucid Dreaming Dangerous?

You've learned about many of the potential benefits of lucid dreaming, but what are the drawbacks? Could lucid dreaming become too much of a good thing? That could be a possibility if you go overboard and sleep away your life and possibly miss opportunities waiting for you. That sounds a little extreme, but seriously, moderation is a good model to help guide you in many aspects of life.

Could a lucid dream be so intense that you could die in the middle of it? When you experience a normal dream, you can experience intense emotions from fear to ecstasy. You probably have woken up more than once with your pulse racing because in your dream you were in eminent danger, perhaps even at the point of death. You haven't died yet from dreaming, and neither has anyone else. Besides, if someone died in a dream, she wouldn't be here to talk about it. Remember, you are in charge of your lucid dream destinies.

Addiction Concerns

Some people can get attached or even addicted to certain patterns in their life. Think of a video game player for a moment. Some become so addicted that they forget about anything else and can lose touch with reality. This happens with online gaming, which can also put the participant thousands of dollars in debt.

In a lucid dream, the "high" of the fantasy can keep someone from trying to find it again. It is possible that some people will seek to have a lucid dream experience as often as possible, making excuses to miss events and withdraw further and further into the fantasy world. When someone gets to this point, she has lost sight of life's big picture. Again, the message here is to approach lucid dreaming as an opportunity to learn a wonderful tool that can help you in life, not help you withdraw from life.

Psychological Concerns

There is a concern that those who have a psychological condition requiring treatment should check with their therapist before attempting to experience lucid dreams. It is important to know consciously that you are experiencing a dream and to have a solid base in normal reality. In other words, when we are dealing with reality in life, we need to be able to measure clearly in our minds how our actions can affect others.

ALERT

Be wary of using drugs to help induce your lucid dreams. Remember, it's important to make sure your conscious mind is fully able to process when you experience a lucid dream. This book encourages a holistic approach to lucid dreaming. The goal is to be able to explore your experiences with complete freedom from any addictive substances.

Finally, imagine what it would be like if your fears kept you from experiencing something that could change your life for the better. There is a danger that the fear of lucid dreams could do just that. It is your willingness to take the risk of succeeding as you read through and try the exercises in this book that can wipe away the danger of failing. Remember that there are no failures connected to lucid dreaming, only varying degrees of success.

The Causes of Lucid Dreams

Why do lucid dreams occur in the first place? By themselves, lucid dreams on average are not a normal occurrence. Researchers have determined that only approximately 20 percent of those queried experience lucid dreams as often as once a month. At the same time, most people have had one or more lucid dreams sometime during their life. This book will help you create exercises to experience lucid dreams on a more consistent basis.

According to David Lohff, author of *The Dream Directory*, your night is divided into different stages of sleep. The first stage begins when you make the transition from being awake to entering sleep. During this transition, there is still a high level of awareness of your physical environment; therefore, it is easy for sleep to be interrupted, bringing you back to a waking state.

Once you have spent adequate time in this transition without interruption, you enter the next stage of sleep. You are now losing contact with your conscious world. You continue to drift deeper into the third stage of sleep, becoming less and less aware of all conscious thoughts and external stimuli.

FACT

It is during the REM stage that most lucid dreams occur as nonlucid dreams. It is the awareness of consciousness in the lightest stage of sleep that can interrupt a normal dream and bring it to the attention of the dreamer. When these conditions are right, the lucid dreaming process can begin.

Stage three is even deeper, and your brain functions at a slower pace. Your heart rate slows, and your body relaxes as you continue into the fourth and deepest stage of sleep. It is in this deepest sleep stage that some people actually get up and walk with no conscious awareness of what they are doing. During this stage, you begin to enter a restless state known as REM before you begin to return to stage one and start the cycle of sleep all over again.

The REM Sleep Stage

The rapid eye movement stage of sleep, known as REM sleep stage, occurs several times a night, with the longest period occurring near morning. Sleep researchers Rugene Aserinsky and Nathaniel Kleitman first identified the phenomenon of REM. Their breakthrough findings were published in the journal *Science* in 1953, and opened the door for dream and sleep researchers to reach new levels of understanding as to what occurs during sleep.

REM stages of sleep account for approximately 20–25 percent of a sleeper's total time asleep over the course of an average night. The heartbeat and breathing patterns change to irregular ones and muscles become more rigid. Some people may actually speak out loud from their sleep during this stage. A signal that the REM stage is beginning can be observed when the sleeper's eyes start to move under their eyelids.

Negative Dream Influences

Not everyone will experience the REM sleep stage the same way. Your physical and mental conditions can affect how your sleep cycles play out. In other words, when you keep yourself in better shape, you may be better prepared for entering a productive REM sleep stage and also increase your opportunity for a lucid dream. Prolonged use of drugs and alcohol can severely affect one's ability to enter a productive dream state.

For some people, certain foods or drink seem to trigger intense dreams, especially if they are consumed closer to bedtime, by not giving the body enough time to fully digest them before sleep occurs. Chocolate, wine, or foods high in starch are just some that can stimulate the heart during the REM period of sleep. One result can be waking up suddenly in the middle of the night with the heart beating rapidly.

Positive Dream Influences

Some herbs are considered to help promote active dreaming. Ginseng, St. John's Wort, African Dream Root, Valerian, and Calea Zacatechichi are just a few of the many different herbs sold to help facilitate lucid dreaming. This book does not endorse any of these or other products, and it is recommended that you consult your doctor or herbalist before trying dream-promoting supplements.

Some people who are affected by mental conditions that inhibit dreaming can find that as their mental health improves, so, too, does their ability to dream. Researchers have found that the REM sleep stage is actually a healthy release for the brain. This is another example of how the sleeper's physical and mental conditions can have an impact on the amount and quality of their dreams and lucid dreams.

Thanks to the work of many scientists and sleep and dream researchers, it has been established that REM plays a very important role in entering a stage of sleep where lucid dreaming can take place. As you have learned earlier, not all dreams are lucid dreams. Still, the conditions need to be right. Not every REM stage will spawn a lucid dream.

Lucid Dreaming on Purpose

Thus far, you have considered what constitutes a lucid dream and the conditions during which one can occur. You have looked at the potential value of using lucid dreaming as a tool to enhance your life. Much of this book will be dedicated to showing you how to develop lucid dreaming techniques to help you achieve the ability to enter a lucid dream state on a consistent and productive basis.

ESSENTIAL

It is always possible for you to experience a random lucid dream that occurs without any attempt to plan it. The key here is to realize what is taking place so that you can consciously work within the dream to effect a positive outcome.

Ryan woke up with the sound of a giant spaceship that was circling overhead. He watched it land in the lake nearby, and soon others joined it, creating an island. Somehow, there was a baby connected to the dream, and it was about to run out of formula. He was afraid of the giant ship, he needed to find food for the baby. So despite his fear, he went to looking for help. This could have been a nightmare, but he ended up making a connection to a higher source of consciousness that he knew would provide him with the "formula" through thoughts in his mind to help others. By facing his fear, Ryan used his lucid dream to tap into some inner wisdom that gave him insights and guidance for his daily life.

Patience is the key to beginning your lucid dream journey. Lucid dreaming may or may not happen overnight. Your mind is different than anyone else's, and the exact way you dream will also be different. It is easy to embrace the one-size-fits-all concept when looking for guidance. The more different "sizes" or techniques you try as you continue on your lucid dream journey, the more you will develop and learn to trust the technique that is right for you.

CHAPTER 2

Lucid Dreaming Through the Ages

In this chapter, you will examine the role that dreams have played in cultures throughout history. From the Aboriginal peoples of Australia to the Egyptian sleep temples to the Romans, dreams have been used for guidance and healing. You will learn that stimulants have been used over time to help search the worlds within the mind. You will hear about the role that contemporary dream researchers Cecelia Green and Stephen LaBerge have played in helping identify and scientifically prove that it is possible to consciously interact with a dream during sleep.

Dreamtime

Since the beginning of conscious thought, man has used his dreams to bridge the gap between his external physical and internal spiritual worlds. One can only imagine the depth of his spiritual connections as he attempted to communicate with the spirit world. Somehow, he learned or knew in his soul how to connect with the wisdom gained in dreams or altered states of consciousness.

Australian Aboriginal mythology refers to the formation of the earth as the "Dreamtime," a period of dreaming in a time before time, when mystical beings came to earth. During that era, the earth was flat and gray, until giant animals on their quest for food and water created the mountains by their digging. This shaping of the land also led to the creation of rivers and oceans.

FACT

The Aborigines believe that Ancestor Spirits contributed to the formation of all plant, animal, and human life, and that the connection still remains today. In other words, it would seem that their ancestors embraced a quantum view of life. Perhaps their dream stories were created in a way similar to today's lucid dreaming.

Aborigines handed down their stories verbally, generation to generation. Even to this day, they have no formal written language. Some 40,000 years ago, the stories began to be developed as a way to teach as well as to guide the Aboriginal people in living their lives. They believed a connection existed between all spirit forms and that there is a *jiva* or *guruwari*, known as a "seed power," contained within the earth that has an energy imprint of all the activities that have taken place on the land.

Other Ancient Cultures

The Assyrians believed that if a dreamer experienced multiple flying dreams he would lose his possessions. The Babylonians thought good dreams were messages from the gods, and bad ones were messages from demons. The *Vigyan Bhairav Tantra* is an ancient Hindu text that gives instructions on how to use consciousness while in a sleep state, indicating that the concept of lucid dreaming has been around for a long time.

Some cultures considered dreaming to be connected to a higher level of consciousness than is achieved during a waking state. Aristotle referred to the concept of lucid dreaming in 350 B.C. when he wrote *On Dreams*, the premise that his consciousness was present in his dreams. Socrates and Plato also looked to their dreams for guidance.

Dream Guidance

The Greeks had dream interpreters to help decipher the visions that their military leaders received in dreams. They also practiced "dream incubation," a technique or ritual often practiced in temples involving drugs to facilitate deep sleep, leading to dreams. Almost every culture has a tradition, myth, or legend going back to a time when dreams were connections to the gods and used for divine guidance.

There seems to be historical evidence to support the idea that along with traditional dreams, a technique similar to lucid dreaming was also employed. In a way, today's lucid dreamers are following in the footsteps of the Ancients that have journeyed through the world of dreams since the beginning of consciousness.

Sleep Temples

Sleep temples, considered to be the forerunner to modern-day hypnosis concepts, were developed and used in Egypt in 3000 B.C., as documented through hieroglyphics on tomb walls. Imhotep, high priest of the sun god Ra, was one of the proponents of the use of sleep temples, also known as dream temples. The sleep temples were used for rituals led by a high priest for purposes of rebirth and healing.

Often, drugs were used to induce the subject into a deep sleep, where they would journey by out-of-body experiences to other realities. Sometimes the subjects would not return from the journey, dying in the process; but for those that did, the experience was like what is considered to be a near-death experience today. There will be a section comparing near-death experiences and lucid dreams later in this book.

Hypnotic Sleep

Those who did return from their sleep travel related stories of feeling terror. In this deep form of trance-like sleep, the subjects seemed to have been able to maintain some sort of a conscious awareness of what transpired during the journey. They experienced a deep somnambulistic hypnotic-like sleep, and even though they were aware, they probably felt powerless to change the direction of their journey.

In a way, the ancient sleep temples were the modern hospitals of that time period. Many of the patients suffered from mental afflictions, and the cures suggested by the priests were often accomplished by the power of suggestion. The power of suggestion is an important tool used to help facilitate lucid dreaming.

Healing Ritual

The Egyptian sleep temples became models for sleep temples created by other countries such as Greece. The Greek god Asclepios was the god of healing, and at one time, there were over 400 sleep temples located throughout the Greek Empire. The priests used the power of suggestion to contact Asclepios through their dreams in a deep sleep state for help in healing. The healing ritual process lasted as long as three days while the priest induced the trance-like sleeping state with chanting and spells.

The Romans also used sleep temples to create trance-like dream states. There has even been evidence found of a Roman sleep temple in England. The Hebrews used similar rituals to bring about healing through their god Kavanah. There is evidence that St. Augustine of Hippo had a working knowledge of lucid dreaming in the early A.D. 400s. Chinese dream temples were a place where the leaders could come to receive knowledge to help them rule.

Tibetan Buddhists

Tibetan Buddhists were known to have used a form of lucid dreaming as early as the A.D. 700s. During that time, Padmasambhava developed the system known as The Yoga Dream State. These concepts have been passed down through the centuries by the Kagyu and Nyingma lineages to the modern-day practice of dream yoga.

Tibetan dream yoga consists of six different stages, according to Evans-Wentz, author of *Tibetan Yoga and Secret Doctrines*. In each stage, the dreamer is given instructions to follow:

- **Stage 1:** Become lucid in the dream.
- **Stage 2:** Overcome all fears of the dream, knowing you cannot be harmed by it.
- **Stage 3:** Consider the dream in relationship to the waking state from the view that both the dream and waking state are actually like an illusion.
- **Stage 4:** Take control of the dream and change the size and weight of objects that would normally be obstructions.
- **Stage 5:** Realize that you have the same control over your physical body as you do objects.
- **Stage 6:** Using images of deities, focus on the mystical state of the *Clear Light of the Void* and be open to receiving revelations.

FACT

Many of the ancient yoga writings known as "transmissions" were derived from deep dream states of connection to the *Clear Light of the Void*. The void is the passageway into the next dimension. Clear light, which is similar to lucidity, is the insight or transmissions that come through this other dimension.

Another method of dream yoga, Zhitro, uses four stages:

- **Stage 1:** Recognize that you are dreaming.
- **Stage 2:** Change the dream.
- **Stage 3:** Build on the dream.
- **Stage 4:** Bring understanding into the dream.

Devoted practitioners of dream yoga view waking life itself as living in a dream or an illusion. In fact, there is a term that describes this philosophy called lucid living. It is a unique way of looking at and experiencing life from a somewhat consciously detached state of consciousness while at the same time being fully aware of both the real and spiritual worlds. If you are interested in investigating these or other yoga dream techniques, there are many reputable yoga studios that would be happy to assist and train you.

Sir Thomas Browne

Sir Thomas Browne (1605–1682), English physician, philosopher, and author of the essay *On Dreams*, stated, "A good part of our sleep is peered out with visions and fantastical objects." In this essay, Browne showed his interest and knowledge of earlier Greek and Egyptian dream culture. He suggested that guardian spirits have the ability to enter dreams to provide "strange hints, instigations, or discourses" for the dreamer. In his book *Religio Medici*, Browne wrote of being able to dream a whole comedy and then "laugh himself awake."

FACT

Browne believed in the existence of witches, and, in a way, may have inadvertently played a role in the Salem witch trials in America. His testimony at the Bury St. Edmunds trial in England in 1662 regarding a similar case was later used as "spectral evidence" influencing a Salem guilty verdict.

French scientist The Marquis d'Hervey de Saint-Denys wrote the book *Dreams and How to Guide Them; Practical Observation*, which was published anonymously in 1867. It contained a report of thirty-two years of lucid dreaming experiences first begun when Saint-Denys was a teenager. At age thirteen, he started a diary as he learned to work with his dreams. He used snapshots of memories in his mind that he consciously integrated into his dream state. It was his ability to recall his dreams that allowed him to produce such a large body of work on the subject.

Saint-Denys's dream work is highly respected by today's researchers. He is considered to be the father of contemporary lucid dream research. Sigmund Freud refers to Saint-Denys's dream studies in his *Interpretations of Dreams* published in 1899. However, the word "lucid" would not find its way into the dream vocabulary world until the early 1990s.

Frederik van Eeden

It was Dutch psychiatrist Frederik van Eeden (1860–1932) who first coined the term "lucid dreams" in his 1913 paper, *A Study of Dreams*. Van Eeden began studying his dreams in 1896. By the time he published his paper, he had collected 500 dreams, 352 of which he thought particularly important. He considered his paper to be a preliminary announcement to a greater body of dream work to come later in his career.

FACT

> Van Eeden categorized his dreams into nine different types. He knew that he would be criticized, but he said, "They would say what I call a dream is no dream, but sort of a trance, or hallucination, or ecstasy." He compared his lack of acceptance to that of the work of Saint-Denys, which was also met with skepticism.

Eeden determined that while in his 352 intriguing dreams in a "normal deep and healthy sleep," he had full recollection of them in his waking life, and he was able to "act voluntarily" even though he was asleep. The sentence that helped define lucid dreams read, "For my part, it was just this form of dream, which I call 'lucid dreams' which aroused my keenest interest and which I noted down carefully." The term caught on and has been embraced by dream and sleep researchers from that time until the present.

Eeden declared in his paper that he knew he was about to experience a lucid dream after two or three nights of flying dreams beforehand. He concluded his paper stating, "We are here, however, on the borders of a realm of mystery where we have to advance very carefully. To deny may be just as dangerous and misleading as to accept."

Psychedelic Period

Throughout history, dream journeying from a waking state has often included the use of drugs in trance-inducing rituals. In fact, Eeden referred to drugs that brought about hallucinations, including cocaine that "produces delicious expectations and pleasant dreams," and alcohol that causes "visions of small white animals."

ALERT

The purpose of this section of the book is not to endorse the use of any drugs but rather to look at a part of history where an attempt was and is still being made to explore the inner recesses of the mind with the aid of mind-altering substances.

In ancient Mayan culture, the shamans used mushrooms to journey into spiritual realms. Many other devices were included in ceremonies throughout the globe. Local seeds, cactus, drinking concoctions, plants, or roots could find their way into the rituals. Other trance-inducing activities might include chanting, dancing, or bright lights.

The Intellectuals

The intellectual world of the early and mid 1900s embraced the use of mind-altering substances to heighten their creative and spiritual initiatives. Writer Aldous Huxley began experimenting with mescaline in 1953, and his experiences were the inspiration for his book *Doors of Perception*, published in 1954. Alan Watts, philosopher and writer, began experimenting with LSD in 1958, and his writing of *Joyous Cosmology* during the 1960s is a statement of his views.

In May 1957, *Life* magazine published a story by Gorgon Wasson, a vice president with J. P. Morgan, entitled "Seeking the Magic Mushroom," an account of his search for and experimenting with hallucinogenic mushrooms in the mountains of Mexico. This story shows that the public had not yet established psychedelic experiences as unacceptable. At Harvard, psychiatrist Dr. Timothy Leary was well known for his experiments with psilocybin, derived from a mushroom from Mexico.

Breathwork

Everything changed in 1966, when psychedelic drugs became illegal. By then they had permeated almost every aspect of pop culture. It would be Doctor Stanislav Grof, author of *Realms of Human Consciousness*, who would take his earlier research on LSD and create the technique Holotropic Breathwork. He established a method of a nonpsychedelic protocol to create similar results in participants as he had achieved through psychedelic means.

FACT

Some of the results from workshops in Holotropic Breathwork include out-of-body experiences and encounters with spiritual beings as well as connections to the greater unconsciousness.

It is evident that the goal of many of the psychedelic researchers of the early and mid-1900s was to expand their understanding of consciousness. How does this relate to lucid dreaming? Many of these types of experiences took the journeyer into expanded states of awareness where they believed they would gain new insights, but they seem to have been somewhat powerless to control their journeys. Consciously engaging in the dream is one of the main goals of lucid dreaming.

Celia Green

Celia Elizabeth Green propelled the topic of lucid dreaming into the mainstream with her book *Lucid Dreams*, published in 1968. Green, born in England in 1935, founded the Institute of Psychophysical Research in 1961, and first took note of lucid dreams while doing postgraduate work on unusual states of consciousness at Oxford. She found a similarity between lucid dreams and out-of-body experiences.

Green found that all metaphoric experiences "have obvious similarities in that they provide a person with a substitute environment which entirely replaces the physical world normally perceived." In other words, both lucid dreams and out-of-body experiences provide mechanisms for individuals to gain insights about life from a different dimension of reality.

OBEs and REM

The difference for Green between lucid dreams and out-of-body experiences (OBEs) was that lucid dreams were much easier to access during laboratory experiments then OBEs. Lucid dreams more often begin from the sleep state, whereas OBEs are often initiated from a waking state, many times as the result of an accident or brought on while experiencing anesthesia. Green also found that OBEs were usually experienced on a larger plane of nonphysical reality, such as traveling long distances, while lucid dreams contained a greater degree of physical reality.

Green is credited with identifying the REM stage of sleep and its connection to potential lucid dream experiences. She also developed the theory that two-way communication could be established through a signaling system between someone in a lucid dream and someone fully conscious. This theory was proven to be valid by other researchers in two separate laboratory experiments.

Lucid Dreaming and Hallucinations

Green has collaborated with British psychologist Charles McCreery since 1964 on the study of hallucinations in lucid dreams, OBEs, and apparitions. An apparition is something that is seen and possibly experienced in a waking state but is not experienced as a reality by others in the same location. In other words, the subject is hallucinating in an altered state of consciousness. Green and McCreery coauthored *Apparitions* in 1975 and *Lucid Dreaming: the Paradox of Consciousness During Sleep* in 1994.

ALERT

Subjects in deep states of hypnosis can experience both positive and negative hallucinations. In a positive hallucination, the subject has the ability to see something that is not physically there. In a negative hallucination, the subject does not see something that is actually there.

Through the study of what a subject may consciously experience in lucid dreams, OBEs, and apparitions, Green and McCreery have developed an understanding of these processes that has helped others understand how to use the power of lucid dreaming in their lives. It is the control of consciousness that gives one the ability to create positive new realities while in states of unconsciousness. The trick is to have a firm grasp on reality.

Stephen LaBerge

As we wrap up our journey back through the practices of various societies and the body of research that has shaped today's concepts of lucid dreams, we come to Stephen LaBerge, one of the giants in the field. LaBerge, born in 1947, began experiencing lucid dreams during his childhood. After earning a bachelor's degree in mathematics, he decided to pursue his lucid dream interest, and his research on the subject began during his PhD work in psychophysiology at Stanford University, where he received his degree in 1980.

Doing experiments on himself, he determined that he could signal to observers while he was in a REM sleep stage. Hooked up to an EEG to measure his responses, he was able to generate a previously agreed upon pattern of eye movements, proving scientifically that he was able to consciously control his actions while asleep. Even though others, such as Allan Hobson, were simultaneously conducting this experiment, LaBerge was the first to scientifically establish that signals could consciously be sent during REM. He eventually developed a system of signaling in Morse code by clenching and releasing his fist.

Scientific Breakthroughs

Besides these breakthroughs in the field of lucid dreaming, one of LaBerge's greatest achievements is the creation of the mnemonic-induced lucid dream (MILD) sleep-induction technique. "Mnemonic" relates to memory use. The development of the MILD technique made it much easier to become aware of dreams and to consciously interact with them.

Subjects enter into sleep by reminding themselves that they will wake up after every dream and remember its contents. Before going back to sleep, it is suggested that they will visualize going back inside of the dream, and being consciously aware as it continues.

The Study of Lucid Dreams

Stephen LaBerge's 1985 book, *Lucid Dreaming: The Power of Being Aware and Awake in Your Dreams*, quickly rose in popularity. In it, he shared his research on the subject, which has helped foster interest and establish the concept that lucid dreams could be a valuable tool to help people create positive changes in their lives. In 1987, he founded The Lucidity Institute (*www.lucidity.com*), whose mission is "to advance research on the nature and potentials of consciousness and to apply the results of this research to the advancement of human health and well-being." The Institute offers a variety of opportunities to become involved in the study and development of lucid dreaming.

Are you ready to become an oneironaut? Oneirology is the scientific study of dreams. Perhaps you are not going to become a dream scientist, but that does not mean that you can't become a student of your dreams. As an oneironaut, you become the captain of your ship of lucid dreams. You will learn and develop the skill to help you navigate through the world of lucid dreams.

CHAPTER 3

Different Ways to Lucid Dream

In this chapter, you will learn about different lucid dream-induction techniques. A dream-induced lucid dream (DILD) starts from a sleep state; wake-induced dream (WILD) begins when the subject is awake; and MILD (mnemonic-induced lucid dreams) are used to increase conscious awareness when a dream begins. You will also consider how suggestible subjects can work with a lucid dream facilitator during an altered state of consciousness lucid-dream experience.

Starting from a Normal Dream: DILD

Dream-induced lucid dreams are the most common ways that people experience lucid dreams. Nearly everyone at some stage in his life has experienced a lucid dream, which is waking up and being aware that you are still in a dream. The percentage of people who consistently experience this type of dream is relatively small. Approximately 20 percent have lucid dreams on a regular basis, which is considered to be one or more a month.

ESSENTIAL

In a DILD, you become consciously aware that you are dreaming, whether or not you are in control of the dream. As you learn to recognize a DILD, you will begin to gain conscious control of it. You just need to remember to be consciously prepared to recognize when and what you are dreaming.

Lucid dreams are usually initiated during the REM sleep stage, a period of deep sleep when a person's eyes begin to move rapidly under his eyelids. During a normal night of sleep, the REM stage will be experienced three or four times with the most intense REM close to the end of the total sleep period. Each time that REM occurs, there is the opportunity for a DILD to take place.

Keep a Dream Journal

Unless you are an experienced lucid dreamer, chances are that any lucid dreams you may have experienced were DILDs or dreams that you consciously knew were happening even though you knew you were still sleeping. It may be hard to remember whether or not some of your dreams were actually lucid. At this point in time, it doesn't make any difference. The real benefit is getting in touch with your dream memories. The more you record your dream experiences, whether recent or past, the more it will help to bring them back to your conscious mind and help you be more alert to upcoming dreams.

Have you ever kept a dream journal? If not, this would be an excellent time to start. Dream experiences have a tendency to disappear from the conscious mind over time. In fact, some fade from memory as soon as the night or sleep period is over. Having a written record of your dreams will help you go back and refer to them at a later date. Dreams that do not make sense when they are first experienced may turn out to be more relevant to your life than first thought.

Another reason to keep a dream journal is that it trains your conscious mind to be aware of when a dream is occurring, which in turn also serves to bring about lucidity in a dream. The more you think about dreaming during the times you are awake, the more you may become aware of your dreams shortly after they have occurred. The more you engage your conscious mind recalling your dreams, the more you will automatically remember them shortly after your dream experience.

Special Category for Lucid Dreams

You may want to make a specific section in your dream journal for lucid dream entries, as well as your daily account of your nightly dream activity. You should record your dreams as soon as you wake up so that you will capture your first impressions. These first impressions may also lead to more details when you review them at a later date. Keeping a record of lucid dreams in both your daily and lucid dream sections will help you establish the regularity of lucid dreams, and the role that lucid dreams play in your life.

Maybe you have volumes of dream experiences already recorded. If you do, you should read back over them to look for any potential lucid dream experiences that stand out. You may find that developing a computer file is the best way to keep a dream journal. If this is the case, make sure you back it up and save it on a second device.

If you can, set aside a little time each day where you can add to your dream journal at a pace that is comfortable for you. Right now, it's all about becoming aware of your dreams.

Random Lucid Dreams

Are dreams really random, or do they have some sort of purpose? If you have experienced only a few lucid dreams in your life, chances are you have thought of them as random dreams that just happen. Many people are not in the habit of paying attention to their dreams. In fact, most don't remember in the morning what they have dreamed the night before.

The fact that you are reading this book indicates that something about dreams, especially lucid dreams, has sparked your interest. In many ways, your dreams are the window to your unconscious mind. The unconscious mind represents about 90 percent of your total mind. When you are asleep, your unconscious mind has the chance to play out what has been going on behind the scenes in your conscious mind. During REM, that time in your sleep cycle where you are in dream mode, your unconscious mind plays out the images it has stored up while your conscious mind was in control.

Your sleep cycle usually repeats itself several times a night, whether you are aware of it or not. Sometimes you have periods in your life where you dream a lot, but other times it seems as if you rarely dream. Remember, your physical and mental condition may have something to do with that, and certain medications can also act as dream blockers.

FACT

Josh had had some memorable dreams in his life, but it wasn't until he was in a six-month period of intense creativity that the dreams became so prolific that he felt he needed to keep a dream journal. Then when that period was over, the dreaming subsided.

When you put together your dream journal, write a little section about your dream history, at least what you can remember of it. As you go through this process, the goal is to prime your memory to help you recall dream experiences that you may have long forgotten. Here are some questions to ask yourself that may help facilitate your efforts:

1. What is the earliest dream that you can remember?
2. What is the most recent dream that you can remember?
3. How many dreams can you remember having in the last month?
4. Are there any notable dreams that stand out to you over the past year? Five years?

5. Was there any time in your life when you experienced intense dream periods?
6. Can you see themes or patterns related to your dreams?
7. What are the most meaningful dreams you have had?
8. Can you remember any lucid dreams?
9. How often do you experience lucid dreams?
10. Is there a pattern to your lucid dreams?

Hopefully, these questions will help you begin to understand the nature of your dreams. You are the judge of whether your dreams are random or not, and especially your lucid dreams. Do you think that perhaps your dreams are being presented to you for guidance and understanding? Is there a greater meaning, something that science might not accept? Up to this point in your life, have your dreams, and particularly lucid dreams, been random?

Planned Lucid Dreams

Wouldn't it be nice to be able to go to sleep knowing that there was a good chance you were going to have an incredible lucid dream experience? Today, thanks to the work of Stephen LaBerge and others, you can learn to do just that. That said, it is good to remember that each person experiences all dreams, including lucid dreams, differently than anyone else. One of the reasons for that is your different mental makeup. It all relates to how you imagine in your mind.

How can you plan to have a lucid dream experience as a part of your normal nightly sleep? You have already taken the first step, which is the desire to dream. Your own motivation is a very important ingredient. Every day when you spend time consciously thinking about dreaming, the more that thought begins to permeate your unconscious mind. You are establishing the habit of dreaming.

Consciously, you should add your intention to remember the contents of your dreams. Say to yourself that you will become aware when you are dreaming and will have a clear recollection of the experience. Tell yourself that when you wake up while or right after the dream has ended, you will remember details of the dream and will record the experience right away.

Tips on Remembering Lucid Dreams

One of the keys to developing your ability for lucid dreaming is to be able to recall your nonlucid dreams. You can start with the goal of remembering at least one dream per night. However, it may take you a little time before you produce consistent memories of your dreams. Remember, it is your desire to work with your dreams that will go a long ways toward accomplishing your dream goals.

Suggest to yourself that you will be able to imagine that the dream is still going on after you have become conscious of it. Awareness of your regular dreams is an excellent launching place to enter into a lucid dream. So when you become aware that you have experienced a dream, try picturing in your mind what is happening. If you are not visual, just recall your dream in a way that works for you. It may be just the emotional feelings of the dream that you are able to work with.

Are you in shape for dreaming? Being in shape means being willing to take care of yourself physically, mentally, and spiritually. In other words, eat healthy or at least be aware of what foods and drink you are putting in your body. You might want to include what you have eaten as a part of your dream journal. Be cautious of foods that are hard to digest in the evening before you go to bed, as they may have an impact on your sleep.

Are you able to and do you get any exercise? It is healthy for the body to get physical activity. Going to bed ready for a sound sleep is also good for facilitating dreams. How do you handle stress? A positive mental outlook can help promote a good night's sleep.

ALERT

If you are having trouble recalling your dreams, you may be sleeping too deeply. If you find that is the case, try setting an alarm clock for the mid- to later part of your sleep period. This may wake you in the middle of or close to a dream experience. It may take a little adjustment for timing.

The longer your sleep period lasts the greater the chance for you to have better dreams. As the sleep period winds on, you are more prone to having a longer REM cycle. That can mean longer-lasting dreams. Dreams that are longer may provide you with more substance to work with. Above all, remember to stay positive and resolved to developing your lucid dream experiences.

Mnemonic-Induced Lucid Dream: MILD

As you can see, experiencing lucid dreaming during normal sleep may be somewhat hit or miss. Under controlled laboratory experiments, LaBerge became aware that there were other ways to induce lucid dreams that proved to be far more consistent. The MILD technique is basically training your mind to become consciously aware while you are sleeping that you are having a dream. The word "mnemonic" is a tongue-twisting word, but think of it simply as memory training. Mnemonics is the use of a system or technique to train the memory to accomplish a specific task. The MILD technique not only works for spontaneous DILDs, but with other lucid dream techniques. The more you practice, the more you will train yourself to remember consciously to be aware when you start to dream during REM.

While researching his own lucid dreams, LaBerge developed the MILD technique. This technique requires the willingness and the ability to focus consciously and precisely on the desired outcome. This is often done when you are going to sleep at the beginning of your sleep period, and is similar to self-hypnosis. If you are familiar with the secret of the Law of Attraction, then you realize the importance of stating clearly what you are asking to attract.

QUESTION

What is the Law of Attraction?
The Law of Attraction is the principle that like attracts like. If you send out a negative thought, you attract negativity into your life. If you send out positive thoughts, you attract positive results. Positive intentions for lucid dreaming attract lucid dreams.

The goal here is for you to become more consciously aware as you prepare for your lucid dream experience. Use the skills you have developed to observe your surroundings to create more powerful wording for your suggestions to yourself. The more you focus on your positive intentions to experience lucid dreaming, the more you will be open to having lucid dreams.

Make a Question Plan

LaBerge recommends a series of daily exercises to help you train yourself to be fully aware of what is taking place around you. He suggests that you create five different questions a day to help sharpen your focus. For instance, you might suggest to yourself that you will make a note the next time you hear an airplane or the sound of a large truck.

You have five different senses, and your observation questions to yourself can be related to any one of them. It could be something you see, feel, hear, smell, or even taste. Remember, this is an exercise in conscious awareness, so be careful not to pick something too common or too remote. Choose something that is likely to be connected to your daily routine.

When you set up a plan to use the MILD technique, you will want to develop a week's worth of awareness questions, or thirty-five of them. It is also a good idea to practice this exercise for a week or two before and continue to use it after you establish your full MILD program.

Autosuggestion

If this exercise and the rest of the MILD technique is hard to focus on, don't worry—there are other ways to help you induce lucid dreams. Probably the simplest technique is the use of autosuggestion. For lucid dreaming, you would repeat that suggestion to yourself before going to sleep. It might read something like, "Tonight when I sleep, I will have a lucid dream." This is a very simple statement and does not require a lot of focus to remember to repeat before drifting off to sleep.

FACT

Emile Coué began using autosuggestion in the early 1900s, which lead to its popularity in fields such as hypnosis. The theory of autosuggestion is that by repeating over and over again a suggestion that is achievable, the mind will accept the suggestion as a reality.

Autosuggestion does not carry the same expectancy as the more intense WILD technique. Just feel that you are going to have a lucid dream. You don't have to set the parameters of when or how it will come into your consciousness. When you are ready, you will just drift off to sleep, open to the reality that you will have a lucid dream sometime.

Starting from a Waking State: WILD

If you are used to meditating or using self-hypnosis, you may want to try the WILD technique of lucid dreaming. Starting from a waking state, you begin to drift off into sleep while continuing to stay consciously aware. As you drift, continue to remind yourself that you will remain aware as you enter sleep and into REM.

The time between being awake and falling asleep is known as a hypnagogic or hypnogogic stage. It is a time when you are still aware of your environment and the thoughts in your mind. As you continue to drift closer to falling asleep, you begin to lose your conscious awareness of your surroundings. The goal of the WILD is to help focus your conscious mind on staying aware as you move through the hypnagogic stage and into sleep.

ESSENTIAL

The goal of the WILD technique is to keep you consciously aware during the hypnagogic stage. By maintaining this awareness when you start to dream, you will be ready to begin a lucid dream adventure. As you progress in this book, you will learn some exercises to help you stay consciously aware as you drift off into sleep.

The WILD technique is very similar to an altered state of conscious technique, except that the goal is to enter sleep, while the altered state technique is to enter into a lucid dream trance. The WILD method is also helpful for lucid dreaming during shorter sleep periods, such as napping during the day. This technique does depend on your ability to easily drift off into sleep, and if you are a natural at that, you may be pleased with the results of a WILD experience.

Waking Up and Going Back to Sleep

Another way of entering into a lucid dream state is from a waking state after a period of sleep. This often happens in the middle of the night or near the end of a long sleep period. Perhaps you have woken up as you were experiencing a dream. All of the emotions and images are still fresh in your mind, so it is possible to reconnect with your dream.

While you are awake and remembering your dream, let yourself imagine that the dream is still going on. If you visualize, see it in your mind's eye as you did when you were sleeping. Go back to a part near the end of the dream and replay it. Experience it and let your imagination keep running beyond the point where you woke up. Suggest to yourself that you are now dreaming again.

Also suggest to yourself that you will fully recall your dream when you wake up again. Once you are consciously aware that you are dreaming, you are free to enter the dream and change it any way you want. You can, if you want, suggest to yourself during the day and before you go to sleep at night that you intend to wake up during a dream and then re-enter your dream as you go back to sleep, being fully aware.

Another way of re-entering into a dream is to wake yourself by setting an alarm. The goal is to wake up during a REM stage and then consciously be aware of going back to sleep. Some people actually stay awake for a period of time to stimulate their conscious minds. They may read, listen to music, or write in their journal. When they are ready, they drift off into sleep, keeping their conscious minds aware and ready to connect with a dream.

Starting from an Altered State of Consciousness

Another technique very similar to WILD is the use of altered states of consciousness to produce lucid dream experiences. The object is to hold onto conscious awareness and move directly into a dream experience using a trance state sleep rather than actually drifting off to sleep. Those who are most successful with this technique are often people who are used to practicing powerful mind-focusing exercises such as meditation, yoga, or self-hypnosis.

Not everyone is capable of entering into a deep state of focus. Some people just have a natural awareness of their environment and have trouble letting go or focusing on a single thought or purpose. For this type of individual, something will usually pull their focus away from entering into a deep altered state of consciousness. People are products of their environment, and for those who have learned to be highly vigilant of their surroundings, focusing on one thought may be difficult.

Conscious Awareness

As you consciously move from your waking state to your trance sleep-like state, you progress through a series of steps, each one moving you deeper into a trance or altered state of consciousness. In order to move on to the next step, it is necessary to accept the reality of the last step. If you suggest to yourself that your muscles are relaxing, then you need to feel that your muscles are actually relaxing. As you accept these suggestions, you are also maintaining a conscious awareness of what you are experiencing as you experience it.

FACT

Hypnotist Harry Arons developed a method of testing how deep into a trance his subjects would go. This technique, known as the Arons Depth Scale, classifies hypnosis subjects into six different categories of trance. Level one is a light trance, like daydreaming, and level six is the deepest trance, where the subject has no conscious awareness.

One of the advantages of staying consciously aware through your induction process is that it may help you set up specific goals during a lucid dream experience. For instance, you may want to work on self-improvement or practice and hone a skill while you are lucid dreaming. The key is patience. The goal is to help you determine and develop the right lucid dreaming technique for you.

Interactive Facilitated Lucid Dreams

Another way to enter into a lucid dream state from a waking state is to use aids to facilitate the process. There was a time when drugs such as LSD were legal, and a small amount could be administrated to a subject to help induce the dream state. Today there are dietary supplements that can be purchased for that same purpose. This book does not advocate the use of anything that alters the mind other than using one's own natural abilities.

There are other tools besides supplements that can be used to help deepen the focus of the participant, including sound and visual stimulation. Music, the sounds of nature, and other recordings provide audio focus for a subject to concentrate on. Visual focus points such as light and mirrors can also help facilitate a WILD.

A subject can listen to a recorded verbal induction from a prepared script. Smells can be used to enhance a subject's state of focus. Emotions can be powerful focus points. The feeling of unconditional love flowing through and over the body can be used to create lucid dream trances. Each person will respond a little differently to sensory stimulation.

Use Some Outside Help

A highly suggestible subject can be induced into a sleep state by an experienced facilitator. The length of time to induce the lucid dream state can be reduced through the use of suggestion. The facilitator can direct the subject's attention and keep him focused on the soon-to-come lucid dream.

ESSENTIAL

The word *hypnosis*, meaning "sleep" in Greek, is actually a misnomer. A hypnotized subject is not asleep but is in a state of heightened focus on every word the facilitator speaks. It is the facilitator's instructions that can help the subject experience a lucid dream while in a hypnotic trance.

When the subject is in a deep state of "sleep," it can be suggested that they are going into REM and will become aware that they are dreaming. Next, the dream becomes a lucid dream. The subject can describe what is taking place in the dream, and it can be suggested that he can manipulate the dream experience in any way that he wants, or the facilitator can set up a lucid dream scenario. Finally, the facilitator can suggest that when he comes back to full consciousness, he will remember everything that took place in his lucid dream as well as feeling any positive effects that may have been experienced.

Not every subject will be able to experience a trance level deep enough to have a meaningful facilitated lucid dream experience. For those who are able, a facilitated lucid dream induction may prove to be a useful and productive technique. The problem with this technique is that it requires someone to assist. The results could be debated as to whether the subject is actually having a lucid dream or just hallucinating in a controlled trance setting. If it can achieve productive results, then it is a technique that may be considered.

CHAPTER 4

Entering a Lucid Dream from Sleep

Here you will begin to make plans for a lucid dreaming experience. You will come to realize the importance of setting clear intentions and the power of the heart when coupled with gratitude and positive expectations. You will learn what to expect when you wake up in a dream and how to prove to yourself that you are actually dreaming. You will know what it's like to be an observer or a participant in a lucid dream.

Setting a Plan

You are now ready to begin putting a plan together to experience lucid dreams during your normal REM sleep. If you haven't started a dream journal yet, this is the time to do it. If you are or already have been keeping a dream journal, that's great; you are right on schedule. Patience is the key.

You may become a proficient lucid dreamer or you may have just a passing interest in the subject. Either way, once you have the knowledge of how to recognize when you are having a lucid dream, you will have the ability to experience it to the fullest. Even if you only have a single lucid dream sometime in your life after you have read this book, you will be prepared to recognize and engage your conscious mind when you become aware that you are dreaming. It is possible that one lucid dream experience could change your life for the better.

ALERT

It may take a little practice to develop your lucid dreaming techniques. You will progress at your own speed. You may find that one method will work better than another one. The reward comes when you begin to start having consistent lucid dream experiences.

The more you focus on your desire to work your dreams with your conscious mind, the greater the probability that you will begin to remember your dreams. Recording and keeping an up-to-date history of your dream experiences is an important step in implementing your plan to experience dreams.

All dreams are important in their own way; some may provide greater insights than others. At the same time, if you have kept a record of what you have dreamed, you may find something you thought insignificant at first to be more insightful than you realized.

Plan for Success

Conscious dream awareness begins with the desire to remember your dreams. The more you think about wanting to become aware and remember what you are dreaming during your waking hours, the more these thoughts will contribute to a new habit of automatic dream recognition. Part of your plan is to train your conscious mind to be aware.

ESSENTIAL

The great seer, Edgar Cayce, viewed thoughts as realities. He said they were either miracles or crimes. In other words, what you send out in your thoughts or intentions are already realities. You don't have to know how your thoughts are going to manifest into reality; by just thinking them, they are already real.

Part of your conscious awareness plan is a positive expectation that you will accomplish what you want to accomplish. Are you familiar with Rhonda Byrne's best-selling book, *The Secret*? If not, you may want to read it or watch the DVD as a part of your lucid dream plan. Simply put, we attract what we send out. Another good DVD on the concept of the laws of attraction is Wayne Dyer's *The Shift*.

Give Thanks

Try adding some gratitude to the plan. Part of your conscious awareness plan can be to think of something that you are grateful for every morning. It is a great way to start your waking day. If you have some sort of belief or faith, you can thank that source. If you do not, just feeling gratitude should do.

Now add some love to your gratitude. Feel what you are grateful for in your heart. Researchers have found that the heart creates sixty times as much energy as the brain. When you feel it, you are sending out a powerful signal. One of the views of quantum physics is that everything is connected. If you have not seen the movie *What the Bleep*, you may want to check it out to help you get an overview and better understanding of the concept of how things are connected to each other. When you feel gratitude in your heart, you are using its power to attract positive results, including successful lucid dreaming.

Here is a little exercise to try. Every day, repeat this phrase first thing in the morning, during the day as part of your daily awareness routine, and especially at night, right before you begin to drift off into sleep: "I am grate-ful that tonight when I am sleeping, I will consciously become aware when I am having a dream." Before, during, and after you say this phrase, feel the gratitude in your heart.

What Are Your Intentions?

It is important to clearly set your intentions about what you expect to accomplish during your sleep. There's an old saying that goes something like, "Be careful what you ask for; you might get it." You may want to tweak your phrase to fit your purpose. Keep it simple and to the point.

Here is a quick reminder list of what is included in your dream-induced lucid dream plan (DILD) so far:

1. Create a dream journal.
2. Start your day by reminding yourself of something that you are grateful for and feel it in your heart.
3. Set your conscious awareness intentions that you are grateful that you will be consciously aware when you start to dream in your REM stage of sleep.
4. Pick four to five things each day that will remind you to be aware of your dream intentions.
5. Repeat your intentions before you are about to go to sleep, feeling cer-tain that you will wake up at the right time.

It is also important, as a part of your plan, to prepare for your lucid dream experience in the best positive way that you can. If you are under a lot of stress, you may not be able to focus on your intentions. If you are on some kind of a "mission" to experience a lucid dream, you may in fact be sabotag-ing yourself. The more you go about preparing for your lucid dream adven-tures with a positive attitude and the more you include others in a dialogue about what you are doing, the better your chance of success. Remember, the more lucid dreaming occupies your conscious, the more your unconscious mind is taking it all in.

Becoming Consciously Aware During the Dream

As you have learned, a DILD originates while you are asleep; you do not wake up until after it is over. The question is, how will you become aware that you are dreaming without waking up? There are some steps you can take to help your conscious mind be more alert to when you begin to dream.

One of the first steps is to include in your intentions that you will become consciously aware that you are dreaming when you begin to dream. The more you remind yourself of this intention, the more you will be ready to recognize when you are dreaming. Even if you did not intend to lucid dream at the time you become aware of your dreaming, you will be able to recognize what you are experiencing. Once you are aware, you have options about what to do next as you continue to dream.

If you are not an experienced lucid dreamer, you may question when you begin to become aware of your dreaming whether you are actually asleep or not. It is sort of like knowing that there is a movie playing out in your dreaming mind, and you are watching it take place. When you become aware and start to think, your conscious mind can take over and the dream starts to fade away.

What if I Wake During My Dream?

You may find that when you first become consciously aware that you are dreaming, you will wake up and the dream will be over. That can happen, especially if you have been training your mind to become consciously aware when you begin to dream. It is exciting to find out that you are actually accomplishing what you set out to do. Your conscious mind may become so aware that you wake up.

When George first learned about and began to recognize that he was having lucid dreams, he tried to control them. When he did that, the dream would disappear. He soon learned to just observe a dream when he first became aware of it and then slowly take control.

It may take a little time to get used to dreaming and being consciously aware without waking yourself up. In the meantime, if you do wake up when you are dreaming, don't worry about it. Just lie there and begin to use the wake up and back to sleep method. Remember to be grateful that you were able to become aware that you were dreaming.

Let yourself imagine that the dream is still going on. As you slowly breathe in and out, focus on the dream and imagine. Suggest to yourself that your conscious mind will continue to be aware as you drift back into sleep and into your dream. Remind yourself that you will fully remember your lucid dream when you wake up.

Confirming That You Are Aware and Dreaming

The question is, how do you prove to yourself that you are actually having a lucid dream? There is a process called a reality check that can help you realize that you are in fact consciously aware and in control of your lucid dream. Your reality check will become part of your dream intentions as you expand your dream consciousness.

QUESTION

What is a reality check?
When someone is consciously aware that he is dreaming, he can hold one of his hands up in front of his face in the dream. Once he has proved to himself that he is in control of his hands, he knows he is in control of his dream.

A reality check starts with doing a repetitive exercise when you are awake. To create a habit, you begin with consciously doing something. Eventually, as you practice the repetition of repeating the exercise, it will become a part of your unconsciousness and recalled to your consciousness when something reminds it to do so.

Lucid dream researchers have found that observations made in real life do not appear the same way in a dream. As an example, if you observe a watch, look away, and look back again while you are awake, the time will appear the same, minus a couple of seconds. If you do the same in a dream, when you look away and look back again, the time will be completely different. If you look at your feet and look away in a dream, when you look back again, the background will be different.

Reality Checks

Here are some exercises you can practice several times a day to help you become aware of what to look for in a dream to prove you are really having a lucid dream.

- **Mirror test.** Every time you look at yourself in the mirror, make a mental note of how clear your reflected image is. Remind yourself that this is the real way that your image is reflected, and that it will reflect the same way every time you observe yourself when you are awake. Suggest to yourself that when you dream, you will be able to observe yourself in a mirror. In a dream, your reflection will appear out of focus or somehow be different, proving to yourself that you are having a dream.
- **Wristwatch test.** Do this exercise several times a day. Look at the watch, note the time, look away for a brief moment, and then look back again. The time will look the same except for a few seconds. Tell yourself that this is real, and suggest to yourself that you will see your watch when you realize that you are dreaming. When you look away and back at your watch in your dream, the time will be different, proving to you that you are dreaming.
- **Breath test.** Another exercise to try is to hold your nose while pressing your tongue on the roof of your mouth, covering the opening where air from your nose can enter your mouth. You will be unable to breathe. Remind yourself that you know this is real. Do this exercise several times a day. When you become aware that you are dreaming, do the same exercise, and you will be able to breathe normally.

You are also free to create your own reality checks. Again, it comes down to how you intend to prove to yourself that you are consciously aware that you are dreaming.

Every dream that you are able to remember and record is helping you increase your conscious awareness. It might take a few nights before you start achieving consistent results, but your ability to recognize that you are having a dream and being able to remember it will become a habit. After a while, it becomes a normal nightly routine.

Observing the Dream

Now that you have learned some ways to prove to yourself that you are actually experiencing a lucid dream, what can you do in the dream? First of all, once you are aware that you are dreaming and you know that the dream is not real, you can do anything you want. When you become conscious that you are experiencing a dream, you know that you are in charge rather than being controlled by the images in your subconscious mind that were in control of creating the dream.

You can decide to investigate what you are dreaming and watch it unfold as if you were in a movie theater. Not only can you watch, you can also control the view. If you become aware that you are dreaming, you can watch the character that you are in the dream from a safe distance. As an observer, you can stay clear of the emotional content of the dream. You do not have to be affected by something that might have a negative smell or listen to displeasing sounds. At the same time, as an observer, you can listen in on conversations without being seen.

FACT

Doris used to get very nervous about traveling to new places. She learned that through her dreams, she could travel to any location before she actually physically visited it. Once she had observed her destination in her dreams, she felt prepared to go there.

You can fly in your lucid dreams and visit anywhere on earth you decide or you could see what it is like to be out in space. You can visit or check up on friends and see what they are doing. You might even connect with your psychic ability and understand how you intuitively know what you know.

Participating in the Dream

Besides being an observer in your lucid dreams, you can also be a participant. Once you are consciously aware that you are dreaming, you also know that because the dream is not real, you can alter it if you want. If it is a nightmare, you can change what is frightening you. How about creating a fantasy? You can give yourself any experience you want while you are lucid dreaming.

ESSENTIAL

Carly can only remember one lucid dream from her entire life. She had a history of nightmares. Then one night she realized she was in the middle of a nightmare and knew she was dreaming. She changed the dream by becoming invisible, calling the police, and having the bad guys arrested. She never had that nightmare again.

Teaching you how you can participate in a lucid dream is one of the major goals of this book. It is your desire to lucid dream, coupled with your patience to become consciously aware, and following this book's exercises that will help you achieve your goals.

The last part of this book will show you how to participate in lucid dreams to bring about positive changes in many aspects of your life. As you are learning, a lot of success can depend on how you consciously set your intentions for your lucid dream experience. Once you find yourself consciously inside of and controlling a dream, you will understand the value you can gain from the experience.

Remembering the Dream Afterward

We've talked a lot about the value of keeping a dream journal. Do you have a section reserved for lucid dreams? Hopefully, you have already started it and have entered any previous lucid dream experiences you can remember. If you haven't done this yet, now is the time to do it.

You may only have one lucid dream to record, or you may have enough lucid dream memories to fill a whole dream journal. Everyone's experiences are going to be different and unique. The way your mind recalls will also determine how you will remember and record what you have remembered. Here are some simple questions to help you as you remember and record your lucid dream experience:

1. What did you see in your lucid dream?
2. What did you hear?
3. What were your emotional feelings?
4. Can you remember touching anything? If so, what did you feel?
5. Did you experience any smells in your lucid dream?
6. Did you taste anything?

Not everyone will remember her lucid dream experience the same way. That is because each person has a different mental makeup. The more you record your dreams, the more details you will remember. Make sure that you give yourself the gift of having enough time to work in your dream journal. It is just part of your dream plan as you develop your habit of lucid dreaming.

CHAPTER 5

Entering a Lucid Dream
from a Waking State

Now you will consider how to successfully enter a lucid dream from a waking state called a WILD. You will learn the importance of setting clear intentions that lead to the creation of a mantra to help transform you into a lucid dreamer. You will get some tips on how to wake up on purpose and go back to sleep and have a lucid dream. You will have the opportunity to create a powerful intention mantra.

Setting Your Intentions

You are now familiar with WILD (wake-induced lucid dreams). There are several different approaches as to how and when you want to experience a lucid dream. You could accomplish this during a naptime rather than your normal longer sleep period. Some people find it easy and refreshing for them to nap daily or on a somewhat regular basis. If you are one of those who are in the habit of taking naps, you may want to try entering a lucid dream during your naptime.

Another way is to maintain your consciousness as you drift off to sleep at night, keeping your conscious mind alert when you begin to dream. This may be the most difficult time to accomplish having a lucid dream experience. You may have had a lot going on during the day, making you too tired to focus on maintaining conscious awareness. There are some techniques you can use to keep your conscious mind alert.

One way is to focus on relaxing your muscles as you drift off into sleep. Start with the top of your head and slowly work your way down to your toes. As you do this, continue to suggest to yourself as you progress down your body that you will relax more and more and stay consciously aware of your muscles. Focus on your intention to drift off into sleep when you get to your feet. Your conscious mind will stay aware while your body totally relaxes and you will begin to sleep, then to dream.

You could also play a round of golf or write a story in your mind. You could count backward from 100 to 0, focusing on each number as you count. You could watch a movie in your mind, and suggest to yourself that while you do, you will stay focused on the movie.

False Awakening

There is an interesting phenomenon that can occur when attempting to experience a lucid dream from a WILD during the night known as a false awakening. This can happen when you think that you remember that you had a lucid dream, when, in fact, you never became consciously aware of the experience. You were actually dreaming that you were having a lucid dream. To avoid false awakenings it is important to clearly set your reality-check intentions.

Wake Up and Get Out of Bed

A third way to experience WILD is by waking up at some point in the night and staying consciously aware as you re-enter your sleep. As discussed earlier, there are a couple of different ways for WILD to happen once you have woken up in the middle of the night. The first way is to wake up and go back to sleep. Another way is to wake up and get out of bed for a period of time before lying back down and consciously going back to sleep.

The reason for this is that you have stimulated your conscious mind. It is much more aware than it would be if you woke up and went back to sleep. The biggest problem with this method is that it may be hard for you to get motivated to do it. Also, there may be other obstacles for this method in your house, such as other people that would be interrupted if you got out of bed and became active in the middle of the night.

Waking up on your own when you are having a dream can meet the same resistance as the morning alarm clock, especially if there is a part of you thinking that you want to stay asleep. You might add to your daily intentions that you look forward to waking up when you dream: "I look forward to waking up and becoming fully, consciously aware that I am dreaming."

ESSENTIAL

Your alarm clock waking time may need to be adjusted to help you find the best time that you experience your REM sleep stage. Make sure that you set your intentions so that when the alarm rings, you will be fully aware of what you are experiencing in your dreams.

If you have been trying this technique for a few nights and are still having trouble waking up to the point that you consciously know that you are experiencing a dream, you may want to set the alarm clock to go off about two-thirds of the way through what you would consider to be your average night's sleep. If that sleep period is eight hours, set the alarm somewhere around five hours after you go to bed. The object is to wake up during your last REM stage of the night—hopefully while a dream is in progress.

Repeat Your Intentions

By setting and repeating your intentions to yourself several times a day, you will be actively engaging your conscious mind with your intentions. Conscious repetition can lead to unconscious responses to help reinforce your desire to lucid dream. In other words, practicing being aware can actually help you become aware.

You may want to write out your intentions so that you can get a clear picture of what you have intended. Once you see what you have written, you can play it out in your mind to get a feel for what you want. Ask yourself if the wording is clear and if your goals can be accomplished. It is important that you believe in what you want to accomplish and also believe that what you desire is going to work. If part of you doesn't believe that you can lucid dream, you may not accomplish what you set out to do.

Creating a Mantra

A lucid dream mantra is a short phrase that contains your intentions and expectations for experiencing a lucid dream. The phrase could be as simple as, "I am grateful for having a lucid dream experience tonight." By feeling grateful, you have set the principles of the Law of Attraction in motion that will help you bring about a lucid dream. The conscious awareness of the desire to dream will help you remember to repeat the mantra several times a day.

QUESTION

What is a mantra?
A mantra can be a phrase, a single word, or even a symbol that, when repeated over and over, helps bring about a transformation for the person repeating it. Buddhists and Hindus use mantras as part of their religions.

Creating a mantra to bring about lucid dreams serves a couple of purposes. By repeating your mantra during the day, you are helping keep it in your conscious awareness. When you repeat it while you are going to sleep, you are using it as part of your induction. The mantra helps you create the transformation when you start experiencing lucid dreams consistently.

The lucid dream experiences in themselves could bring about a major transformation in your life. That transformation could come physically, spiritually, mentally, or emotionally. Your transformation can begin when you clearly state and repeat your intentions as a mantra.

Repeat Your Mantra

This brings us back to the importance of repeating your mantra during your hypnagogic state of drowsiness between being fully awake and asleep. It is equally important to believe what you are saying and feeling. A mantra can be a very powerful transformation tool when used to its fullest extent.

You don't have to go around all day repeating spiritual phrases out loud for a mantra to work for you. When you set a goal of becoming consciously aware of five different situations you normally experience each day, such as seeing a red car, say to yourself, "Whenever I see a red car today I will be grateful that I will experience a lucid dream tonight."

Here are some suggestions as you prepare to write down your intentions to help create your mantra:

- Decide when you want to experience your WILD.
- Decide which reality test you want to use to prove that you are consciously aware that you are dreaming.
- Choose five different daily reminders to keep your conscious mind aware of your goals for WILD.
- Think of the imagery you want to use with your mantra.
- Imagine yourself actually completing your intentions.
- Ask yourself if your goals are realistic and achievable.

If there seems to be some question about being successful, rework your intentions until any obstacles, at least in your mind's eye, have been overcome. The more clear and concise you are in establishing your goals the greater the chance to create a powerful mantra.

Drifting Off

Have you ever had one of those nights when it seemed you didn't sleep at all and yet you failed to hear the clock strike every hour? It's like you were wide awake and yet you were also very relaxed. You may have been doing a lot of thinking and at the same time drifting off occasionally. Still, your conscious mind was aware and thinking, but chances are you weren't focused on staying alert for a lucid dream.

The hypnagogic state is a key factor in whether you will have a successful WILD experience. It is important for you to maintain a connection with your conscious mind during this period by continually reminding yourself of your mantra. The goal is to be consciously aware of moving from one state to another.

You will enter your hypnagogic state differently depending on which WILD experience you choose. Also, there is the factor of how stimulated your conscious mind is before you drift off. If you have had food or liquid with stimulants like chocolate or caffeine, you may find it harder to shut your brain off. Stress would also be a deterrent. This is especially true if you want to enter a lucid dream from a nap or when you first go to bed.

These may be good reasons for setting your intentions to experience a WILD in the middle of the night. When you wake up, especially if you do not get out of bed, you may maintain a partial hypnagogic state. To maintain your awareness, constantly remind yourself of your intentions by repeating and emotionally feeling your mantra. The way that you have worded your mantra will have an effect on how your lucid dream experience will unfold.

Being Aware of the Process

So how do you consciously stay tuned in to the process of experiencing a WILD? It may take some practice to accomplish this. Perhaps you have taken part in activities in your life that have prepared you to do that.

Have you ever studied while listening to music or watching television? Some people need complete silence to study or read while others can't focus when it is quiet. Some people can't sleep unless there is sound in the background while others can't sleep if there is any sound. Everyone focuses differently. The goal is to identify how you focus so that you can keep your conscious mind aware while you are drifting off to sleep. Knowing how you fall asleep may relate to how you were able to focus on learning.

FACT

In hypnosis, "flooding" is sometimes used to create an altered state in someone with an active thinking mind. Flooding is a form of sensory overload where the conscious mind is given so many sensory stimulants at once that it cannot focus on any of them. Then it can focus on suggestions or intentions.

If you are experienced at meditation or yoga, you have learned to focus. Self-hypnosis is another way to create an altered state and yet stay focused with your conscious mind on the environment around you. You may have been or still are a good athlete and know what it's like to be in the "zone." You may have another skill or ability that helps you maintain a relaxed focused state.

Take a little time to think about how you are able to maintain focus in other parts of your life that are not stressful for you. Knowing yourself will help you keep a conscious focus as you make a transition from a waking state into a lucid dream. The goal is to identify and understand how you can use what you may do naturally or have learned to use in other aspects of your life that will help you experience a WILD.

Testing the Reality of the Lucid Dream

Testing the reality of a lucid dream from WILD is the same process as for a DILD. The purpose is to prove to yourself that you are actually dreaming. Remember that dream researchers like Stephen LaBerge have proved in scientific laboratory tests that when a dreamer consciously does an exercise in a dream as she has done in her waking state, it will not look the same. When the dreamer knows this, she also knows that she is having a dream and the dream is not reality.

It is possible to wake up remembering that you had a lucid dream. The details are clear to you. The problem is that, in reality, you were dreaming that you were having a lucid dream and not having a real lucid dream. How can you tell the difference? If you don't test the dream, you may not be able to tell whether it was real or not.

This is why it's important to have a daily routine of reminding yourself to observe reality, such as the hands or numbers of a clock. Those five different things to observe each day are the key to keeping your mind focused on reality. Perhaps one of your goals is to be aware the next time a dog barks. Say to yourself, "The next time I hear a dog bark I will look at my watch, look away, look back again, and when the clock looks the same, I know that this is real."

All of this awareness may sound like a lot of work to you, but the effort will be well worthwhile, and once you get into a routine, it will become a habit. Remember, to create a habit, you start by conscious awareness of what you are doing or thinking until it becomes part of the unconscious mind. Good efforts can create good habits.

Coming Back to a Waking State

How do you prepare to come back to a waking state after a WILD experience? Of course, this depends on whether or not you experience your WILD during a nap, the first of the night, or after you have awakened from sleep. The nap itself is usually only a short period of time, so you will probably wake up after, or not long after, you have finished the dream. The memory of your dream should be fresh in your mind.

You can consciously remind yourself during the day and before you drift off into sleep that you will wake up and remember your dream after you have finished it. This may take a little time to program yourself to do. You might say to yourself as a part of your dream mantra, "After I have finished my lucid dream I will wake up and remember it fully."

ALERT

If you don't make a conscious effort to remember your dreams, they may slip away unnoticed. Earlier dreams will be harder to remember than later dreams. Therefore, if you want to experience WILD at the beginning of your night, you will need a method to remind yourself to wake up and remember what you have dreamed.

The other way to wake up after you have experienced a lucid dream is to set an alarm to wake you an hour and a half to two hours or so after you have started your sleep period. The exact time to set the alarm can be determined by how long it generally takes you to experience WILD. The goal is for you to wake up while you have a fresh memory of your lucid dream in your head. Of course, not all dreams are going to be lucid when you try WILD. That's okay, but don't forget to record all your lucid dreams in your dream journal.

If your WILD is toward the end of your sleep period, you may have a clear memory of your experience when you wake up in the morning. You can include this statement in your intentions. The main thing to remember when you come back to a waking state is to record at least some information for your dream journal as soon as possible. You may not want or need to write the whole dream down right away. Key words, thoughts, or other impressions can act as memory prompters when you have the opportunity to write a more detailed account later.

Remembering the Results

Everyone will remember his dreams differently. You may be able to experience the whole dream over and over again, and perhaps even be aware of more details later on than right after you experienced it. As you mull over your dream experience in the next few days afterward, be prepared to make note of any additional information that might come into your mind relating to the dream.

You are constantly taking in information through your five senses: sight, sound, touch, smell, and taste. Much of the time, you aren't consciously aware of what your senses are doing. For instance, your eyes are like a camera; everything you see is recorded through them and the information is stored in your unconscious mind. Think of your unconscious mind acting as the data storage in your computer. Here are some hints to help you remember your dreams:

1. Record a brief summary of the whole dream, including how it began and how it ended.
2. Next, focus on the most vivid scene.

3. Make note of what you are seeing, hearing, feeling, smelling, and tasting.
4. If the dream was lucid, record your reality check.
5. Were you active or just an observer in the dream?
6. If you were active, what did you do?
7. If you changed the dream, how did you change it?
8. What time period was the dream set in?
9. Was there a theme to the dream?
10. What did you learn from the dream and how does it apply to your life?

You may come up with other suggestions to help you remember. It all comes down to becoming consciously aware of what goes on in your dreams. Don't try to force yourself to remember—that can be counterproductive. Just remember to be grateful in advance that you will fully remember your dreams.

Stored Memories

We have information in our unconscious minds that we don't consciously remember is there. You retrieve your unconscious information in two ways. The first way is by consciously searching for information regarding something specific. The second way is that something you are currently experiencing connects with information in your unconscious mind, which is sent up to the surface of your conscious mind, and you are made aware of it.

FACT

Ron had a dream where he saw his deceased father pacing back and forth outside of his mother's house. A year later when his mother died, Ron recognized that he had been shown in his dream that his father would be there to meet her.

It is possible you have had such an incident, when something happening in the moment reminds you of the memory of a dream relating directly to what you are currently experiencing. All of a sudden, you have a flash of recognition that you already know or have insights about what is taking place around you. Most of these types of dream memories are related to regular dreams and are not necessarily lucid dreams.

Intention Exercise

It's time for you to write a lucid dream intention exercise that can become your mantra to attract lucid dream experiences. Even though it seems as if there is a lot to think about when preparing for a lucid dream experience, your mantra does not have to be long and complicated.

These are the key points you should cover when writing your intentions:

- **Goal.** "Tonight, I look forward to experiencing a lucid dream."
- **Awareness.** "I will stay consciously aware as I experience my lucid dream."
- **Reality check.** "I know it is real when the clock has a different time when I look away and look back."
- **Remember.** "When I wake up, I will remember every detail of my dream."

Let's see how you could take those four points and create a mantra; the goal is to combine and create a single sentence that is easy to remember. "Tonight I will be consciously aware as I drift into my lucid dream, will know it is real when I look at the clock face, and will fully remember my dream afterward."

Now you should try putting together your intentions to create a mantra that is right for you. Remember to feel the power of gratitude and love in your heart when you repeat your mantra. Be clear and to the point. Repeat this to yourself as you are drifting off to sleep in your hypnagogic state.

You will learn to fine-tune your lucid dream mantra as you develop your abilities. Remember, the more you engage your conscious mind in lucid dream awareness the greater chance you have for success. It's time to give experiencing a WILD a try.

CHAPTER 6

Altered States of Consciousness

Here you will learn how to use an altered state of consciousness to have a lucid dream experience. You will understand the role of a facilitator in inducing a lucid dream trance while you are in an altered state. You will hear about the sleeping profit, Edgar Cayce, and finally, you will have a chance to try an altered-state lucid dreaming induction. You may find that you can have the experience and results of a lucid dream from an altered state of consciousness trance.

What Is an Altered State of Consciousness?

An altered state of consciousness is a natural phenomenon that we experience all the time. Our minds are constantly on the go. It is hard to hold a steady focus for an extended period, at least for most people. Even when you are able to focus on one point of interest, you are actually in an altered state of consciousness.

Think of a camera lens for a moment. The old-fashioned box camera had one lens, and you had no way to change the focus; you just pointed and took the picture. You may have learned to live your life in a less complex way, which lets you clear your mind and focus easily on a single point of interest.

You may be like a camera with lenses that need to be focused to produce clear pictures. There is a lot more to think about when using this type of camera. Your mind may consider the angle, light, and focus as well as what lens you want to use. You are creating mini altered states during the time that you are preparing to take the picture.

Focusing Your Thoughts

Your mind is constantly flipping back and forth between three different tenses: the past, the present, and the future. In one moment, you may be remembering something you did a few hours ago. In the next, you may be focused on something you are doing or watching. Then you might think about something you hope to be doing in the future.

FACT

A hypnotist will often ask his subject to focus her eyes on a single point of interest and then slowly let them go out of focus. At that point, the subject's focus is being shifted to the hypnotist's words. As her eyes go out of focus, she is beginning to center her attention on the hypnotist's suggestions.

Every one of your thoughts is creating images in your mind through your five different senses. Each image you experience in your mind is an altered state of consciousness. It could be a positive state or it could be a negative one. That is why it is good to resolve stress as best you can because it creates a negative altered state of consciousness and can take your focus away from lucid dreaming.

It's Not Hard

An altered state of consciousness is as simple as daydreaming. In fact, the hypnagogic state between being awake and asleep is an altered state of consciousness. You can consciously create altered states of consciousness for yourself with meditation or self-hypnotic trances. Your trance level depends on your ability to focus on a single point of interest. That is why hypnotists use devices such as strobe lights or a spinning spiral disc.

When you use a self-hypnotic induction or are facilitated by another person or a sound recording, you are creating a deeper and more focused altered state of consciousness. Using this technique for lucid dreaming may help you develop a greater success rate. If you are not experienced at creating deeper altered states of consciousness for yourself, don't worry. As you progress through this book, you will be shown how to be successful.

Setting Goals for the Lucid Dream Trance

By now, you should have a good idea of how to set your lucid dream goals and state them in your intentions. As you progress through this book, you will find that you are constantly honing in and focusing more and more on how to consistently experience lucid dreams. That should be part of your long-range goal.

You may be new to the concept of lucid dreaming or you may already be skilled in the subject. This book will help you become a student of lucid dreaming. You'll find that there is a lot of goal setting involved, but that's not different than any other aspect of life. You are always setting and resetting goals. You need achievable goals to help you get to the big goal of complete lucid dreaming success. Don't lose sight of your daily goals because they are equally as important as the big goal of total success.

Beginning Concepts

The first goal for entering into a lucid dream trance is to become experienced in creating an altered state of consciousness. If you are working with someone who can help you into an altered state such as a hypnotist, then all you have to do is let him guide you. If you are on your own, you are actually learning to become your own hypnotist.

The goal of experiencing a lucid dream from a deeper altered state of consciousness than that achieved in a hypnagogic state is not complex, but you need to keep honing your focus in on the dream while maintaining a conscious awareness. It is quite possible that you will find that entering a self-hypnotic altered state is very useful in many other areas of your life.

Self-Induced Altered States

To begin to enter a self-induced altered state of consciousness, simply focus on your breathing. Take a deep breath that is comfortable for you, and slowly exhale. As your breathing slows down, your mind may begin to empty. When you focus on a lot of thoughts, you may be concentrating so hard on what you are thinking that you forget to breathe. Shallow breathing can deprive the body of oxygen and make it hard to focus on just relaxing.

ALERT

Today's stress brings out our natural instinct of flight or fight. Early man developed this ability for survival. However, it can be detrimental to your health if your constant focus is centered on something that is stressful. Our stress warning system was developed for short-term situations, not the long-term conditions often faced today.

That is why it is important to remember to breathe. One of your first goals or intentions when you are entering into an altered state of consciousness should be to begin to relax when you start focusing on your breathing. In fact, as you learn to relax, you will probably find that you enjoy it. Once you have learned to expect the enjoyment, just the thought of deeper breathing will help you anticipate the positive experience you will have when you are doing it.

Future Pacing

There is a term in hypnosis called future pacing. What it means is that you are suggesting to yourself that you will have a certain experience when a specific action begins. By expecting to experience the positive benefit of relaxing when you start to focus on your breathing, you are giving yourself an expectation of what will happen to you when the process begins. Future pacing helps you narrow your focus on deepening your altered state of consciousness.

By using future pacing when you are writing your self-induction script, you will create stronger intentions to help you focus. Once you get used to the concept of future pacing, it will become easier and easier for you to enter into a self-induced altered state of focus. In fact, once you become accustomed to the process and have created a method that is right for you, the moment you begin to focus on your breathing, you enter into a deeper altered state of consciousness in a shorter amount of time. What you will be doing is creating an expectation that the next time you start a self-induced altered state induction, you will automatically slip easily back into your trance.

Edgar Cayce

Have you ever heard of Edgar Cayce (1877–1945)? If you haven't, you may want to read *There Is a River* by Thomas Sugrue. It tells the story of Edgar Cayce, who was born on a tobacco farm in Kentucky and devoted much of his life to using his unique psychic gifts to help others. He received psychic information through his dreams and was able to interpret other people's dreams.

His body of work includes more than 14,000 readings that were all recorded, categorized, and are still being used for guidance by many people today. His legacy is being carried on by the Association for Research and Enlightenment (A.R.E.) in Virginia Beach, Virginia.

The Source

Cayce learned that he could put himself into a deep altered state of consciousness and connect with a universal source that brought him information, which proved to be true over and over again. By the end of his life, he had received thousands of requests for readings from people all over the world. Many were from the relatives of soldiers in World War II who were concerned about the welfare of their loved ones.

FACT

In his hypnagogic trance state, Cayce would travel out to a source or go to the address of the subject he was reading for, especially if it was a health reading. When asked about the subject, he would often answer, "Yes. We have the body." His readings covered many topics including health, life purpose, predictions of the future, and past lives.

When it came time for a reading, Cayce would loosen his tie, lie down on a couch, and put himself to sleep. There would be others in the room with him, including his stenographer, Gladys Davis, and quite often his wife, Gertrude, who would conduct the session and ask questions. As Cayce entered into sleep, his breathing would slow down, signaling that he was ready to receive and answer questions.

The Channel

Once induced into his deep sleep state, Cayce was able to respond to questions. At this point, he released his conscious awareness, and when he came out of his sleep, he had no knowledge of what had transpired during the session. It appears as if he became a channel for a source somewhere out there in the universe. He often used the word "we," indicating that he was not alone. He would visit a place known as the Akashic Records, where he could read about the history of a soul and explain why the subject faced various conditions in his current life that were impacted by actions from his past lives.

Cayce's method for entering into his altered state of consciousness is similar to the techniques described for entering a lucid dream from an altered state of consciousness. Remember, in the early 1900s, there wasn't a large body of research on lucid dreaming. If Cayce was alive today, perhaps Stephen Laberge and other lucid dream researchers would have been able to study him to help understand what relationship sleep may have had with his altered state of consciousness.

Guided Altered State

It is possible for someone else, such as a hypnotist, to guide you into an altered state of consciousnesss that creates the same or similar experience as a lucid dream. Just as you might be a natural lucid dreamer without any type of training who knows how to consciously interact with your dreams, you might also naturally enter into deep hypnotic states. It all depends on your ability to focus on your imagination. The more real your images become the deeper you will go into a trance.

A hypnotist is actually a facilitator to help guide you into an altered state of consciousness. You are creating the experience yourself with the suggestions of the facilitator. It is possible for you to facilitate your own altered state of consciousness, but it may be easier for someone else to do that for you. The benefit of working with someone else is that you do not have to remain as alert as you would if you were doing it all by yourself.

The Power of Suggestion

A facilitator can use the power of suggestion coupled with future pacing to help induce you into a lucid dream experience. Once you have entered into a deep altered state of focus, the suggestion can be made to you that you will now find yourself in a lucid dream, fully aware and able to move throughout the dream and make changes if you wish. The facilitator can suggest that you dream about a predetermined topic or that you will experience just the right lucid dream for you at that time.

Once you know what a lucid dream is, the facilitator can suggest that you will experience a lucid dream and be fully able to be consciously aware of and interact with it while you are in your altered state of consciousness trance. It can also be suggested that when you come back to full consciousness, you will remember all the details of the lucid dream you experienced.

You may not be able to determine whether you had a lucid dream or were in a hypnotic trance, but it could be said that you experienced a lucid dream while you were in an altered state of consciousness.

ESSENTIAL

Basically, all hypnosis is self-hypnosis. That means it is the individual who creates a trance, not the facilitator or hypnotist. Another word for hypnotist is "operator," and his role is to offer suggestions that help influence the trance that the individual creates. If the individual resists the suggestions, they do not enter into a trance.

Benefits of a Facilitated Dream Trance

There is one major benefit to a facilitated altered-state lucid dream trance: the facilitator can also interact with the lucid dream. You can provide a running commentary on what is taking place while it is happening, and he can offer suggestions that might help provide much more information on the lucid dream than you would normally bring back when you come out of your dream state.

A trained facilitator or hypnotist has the ability to recognize what you may need to experience in a lucid dream trance. He can set up scenarios for the dream and guide you through your experiences. He can also help you stay in a lucid dream trance where you, by yourself, might come back to the surface of your mind before you got the full benefit of the lucid dream experience. Of course, you do not have to have a specific goal to have a lucid dream-trance experience. You can enter a lucid dream trance just for the experience itself.

Speaking from an Altered State of Consciousness Lucid Dream

As long as there is a connection between the facilitator and the subject, the subject will be able to respond to the facilitator's communication. There is a point after the subject has been induced into an altered state of consciousness or hypnagogic state when interaction with the subject ceases and she drifts off into sleep. Some people listen to recorded voice suggestions at night to help them sleep. The last suggestion she hears might be something like, "As this recording ends, you will drift off into a restful, relaxing sleep."

When a hypnotized subject has been given the suggestion that she is having a lucid dream experience, she still maintains contact with the facilitator of the session. She can be asked questions about what she is experiencing and hear suggestions to change the images in the dream. Just as in any other lucid dream, the subject can be instructed to tell herself that her experience isn't real, and therefore she can change it any way she wants. Because the facilitator is monitoring or in control of what the subject is dreaming, he can suggest the outcomes that are best for the subject.

FACT

Skilled past-life facilitators can create altered states of consciousness that guide the subject into memories of past lives and move them around in the life to understand how that life may have impacted their current life. This experience can help resolve issues that can create positive changes in the subject's life.

As an example, a facilitated altered-state lucid dream could be a valuable experience for someone dealing with nightmares. With a WILD or DILD, the subject would prepare for a lucid dream experience and then be ready for it when it happens. In a facilitated altered state, a highly suggestible subject can have a lucid dream experience on the first attempt that has a good chance of resolving the nightmare. In fact, a suggestion can be given to the subject at the end of the lucid dream imagery that they will not experience the nightmare again.

Remembering the Experience

If you are in a deep altered state of consciousness, can you remember your experiences? The answer is yes, if you are given a suggestion that you will recall what went on while you were in the altered state. Some subjects that lose total contact with their conscious minds while in an altered state may have no memory of the events when they come back to full consciousness. Some will have partial memories with more details coming within a period of time, depending on the depth of the trance.

You should always be given positive suggestions as you come out of your altered state of consciousness. The facilitator might suggest:

When you come back to full conscious awareness, you will feel positive and relaxed. You will fully remember your lucid dream experiences without being affected by anything that may have seemed negative. You will understand how you were able to make any positive changes that may have been needed in your dream. You feel positive and relaxed and fully aware of your surroundings.

The suggestions should be designed to be positive and supporting. The wording varies according to the lucid dream goals and experience. It is important to word them so that you will fully remember the lucid dream experience in a way that, if there were negative situations, you will not be impacted by anything you imagined during the dream. Because you will be very focused on the facilitator's words, careful consideration needs to be given so that you will respond as intended.

ESSENTIAL

It can be suggested to a hypnotized subject that they will not remember anything they experienced when they wake from an altered state. That memory can easily be restored by another suggestion to remember. It can also be suggested that over the next few days the subject will remember more details as the information in the experience is processed.

You need a little time to adjust to your surroundings when you come out of an altered state. Perhaps you have had a dream that was so intense that when you woke you weren't sure where you were. This can be especially disconcerting when something causes you to wake up suddenly. The same thing is true when you come out of an altered state of consciousness.

Altered-State Induction

Here is an altered-state induction designed to help facilitate a lucid dream. You can customize it to fit your dream intentions and goals. You can write your own script or use this one. You could also record it and listen to it when you want to experience a facilitated altered-state lucid dream. Remember, at any time you want or need to, you can always open your eyes and come back to full consciousness feeling relaxed, refreshed, and positive.

ESSENTIAL

If you choose to record a script for yourself, read it slowly and give yourself time to experience the suggestions. You can modify it any way that works best for you. You can and may want to change the wording as you gain experience writing your scripts.

Lie down in a comfortable position, and when you are ready, take a comfortable deep breath and slowly exhale. With each breath, you may feel yourself relaxing more and more. For a moment, focus on something that you are grateful for and let yourself feel this gratitude in your heart. As you continue to breathe in and out, feeling gratitude, feel yourself opening up to experiencing a lucid dream.

Let your eyes go out of focus, and when you are ready, let them close. As you continue to breathe in and out, you are relaxing more and more. You may feel the muscles in your body relaxing, and if you feel one stiffen up, you may relax it and go deeper and deeper into your positive altered state of consciousness. You feel gratitude in your heart as you focus on your muscles relaxing all the way from the tip of your head down to the bottom of your feet. In a moment or so, you will hear yourself being counted from five down to zero. (Note: If you are uncomfortable going downward, then count yourself upward.)

5. You are beginning to drift off into a relaxing altered state of consciousness. By the time you get to zero, you will be consciously aware as you enter into a sleep-like state where you will experience a lucid dream. With each breath, you will relax more and more as you go deeper and deeper, fully focused on these words. You feel positive and relaxed.

4. You are going deeper and deeper. By the time you get to zero, you will be in a deep altered state of consciousness fully aware of your lucid dream. You are relaxing more and more.

3. By the time you get to zero, you will be experiencing a lucid dream and will be fully aware that you are dreaming. You will know it is only a dream, and you have the ability to change it in any way you want. You feel positive and look forward to your lucid dream.

2. You are going deeper and deeper into your altered state of consciousness. Soon you will be at zero and in your lucid dream. You will test the reality of the dream and know it to be a dream. You may change it any way you wish. You are drifting deeper and deeper, still focused on these words.

1. On the next count, you will be in a deep altered state and fully, consciously aware of your lucid dream even as you are in a deep sleep. You feel safe and secure, and ready to experience your lucid dream. In a moment, you will be in your dream.

0. Let the images of your dream come into your mind's eye. As you sleep, you are aware of what you are dreaming. As you do a reality check, you know that it is a dream, and it isn't real. You have the ability to change it in any way you want.

Take some time to experience your lucid dream. When you are ready to come back to being fully awake, you will slowly do so. You will fully remember your lucid dream experience and will be able to write it clearly in your dream journal. You will feel relaxed, rested, positive, and looking forward to your next lucid dream experience.

CHAPTER 7

Out-of-Body and Near-Death Experiences

In this chapter, you will learn what unplanned or spontaneous out-of-body experiences (OBEs) are as well as how to plan for experiencing one during a lucid dream. You will consider what a near-death experience (NDE) is and compare lucid dreaming experiences to OBEs and NDEs. Finally, you will learn about remote viewing, have the chance to try developing intentions for an astral-travel lucid dream, an OBE lucid dream, and an OBE altered-state lucid dream trance.

Unplanned Out-of-Body Experiences

Have you ever had an unplanned out-of-body experience? Before you answer that question, let's understand what an OBE is. Simply defined, an OBE happens when you become consciously aware that your perception has shifted to a vantage point from outside of your body. Researchers have determined that between 10 and 20 percent of the population has experienced an OBE sometime during their lives. Of the people who have, a large majority of the experiences were while the individual was in some stage of rest, close to being asleep or dreaming.

Perhaps you have had a dream where you were flying, without a body or with a very light body. The Theosophical Society, founded in 1875 by Madame Blavatsky, includes in its doctrine that we have more than one body. In other words, you may appear in an astral body when you experience an OBE. So essentially, you may or may not sense that you are in some physical form when you are aware of a floating sensation.

FACT

Lisa's first OBE occurred when she was a teenager. She was participating in a group meditation when she suddenly found herself floating up and out of the room. She became frightened and confused and pulled out of the experience, back to full consciousness. Fortunately, someone in the group was able to explain to her what had happened.

Spontaneous or unplanned OBEs can happen at any time in several different ways. Even though the majority of experiences happen when the body is at rest, they can also occur when the person is fully awake. OBEs have even been reported to happen while an individual was operating a motor vehicle and suddenly found themselves above it as it moved along. An OBE can also take place while the person is simply walking. The evidence seems to support that many of the incidents take place while the individuals are in some sort of altered state or light trance.

What Are They Like?

Most of the experiences happen visually in visual images, while some also include sound. One view is that an OBE is actually a form of hallucination, a figment of the mind. An OBE can begin with a rush of sound, a vibrating feeling, or the sensation of everything going blank. There is often the feeling of being snapped back into the physical body when the OBE is over. Typically, a spontaneous OBE lasts only a few seconds, and the person can usually continue what they were doing without any interruption.

ALERT

Unplanned OBEs can happen during a time of stress or impending danger. The individual may suddenly find that he is dealing with it from a different plane. He could be above the action or experiencing it in slow motion. These types of OBEs might happen on a more frequent basis after going through some sort of near-death experience.

Jason, who survived being struck by a car, observed that in the years afterward he had more than three different OBEs that occurred during times of potential danger. One was when a moose crossed the road right in front of him, a second time was when a car crossed the centerline heading right for him, and a third was when someone ran a stop sign. He has also had several experiences where he felt a vibration and spinning in his head while talking with someone else, and, at the same time, an awareness that he was on some sort of astral plane perceiving it all from above.

Have You Had One?

Take a moment and consider whether or not you have had one or more OBEs in your life. Think about your dreams first. Have you ever had a flying dream? Have you ever had the feeling of being snapped back into your physical body during a dream experience? Have you ever experienced an OBE during a meditation or while in a relaxed state? Have you ever felt a vibration or brief loss of focus during a conversation or during some sort of activity such as walking?

Near-death experiences would come under the category of an unplanned OBE. They can spontaneously set off an OBE and can happen during a physical, mental, or spiritual situation.

Some people have an OBE when having a spontaneous past-life regression. An experience like this can happen when something triggers a soul memory that pulls you into an altered state of consciousness connected to a different time period. You may suddenly see that your surroundings look different or that people are dressed differently. You may even experience sounds and smells near you that are not obvious to others. It is like you stepped into some sort of time warp.

OBE Tendencies

When you are in a lucid dream, you can have an OBE. As mentioned earlier, a dream where you find yourself flying is one of the most common types of OBEs. It is also been determined by researchers that people who have frequent lucid dreams also have more OBEs. The evidence seems to indicate that people who have an above average ability to create strong images in their minds are good candidates to have more lucid dreams and OBEs. They also have a tendency to go into deeper altered states of consciousness.

As you can see, there are many ways to have an OBE. Are they real? You are the one that knows what your experience was like. If your OBEs allow you to take away positive insights that you can use to help yourself and others, then that is incredible. Knowing in your heart, regardless of what others think, may be a great source of comfort as you journey through life.

Planned Out-of-Body Experiences

Some people use OBEs as a part of their spiritual rituals. In ancient sleep temples, participants would journey into other realms. Edgar Cayce was out of body when he gave readings. He was able to actually go to the physical location of his subject, tell what the weather was, and scan the subject's body, explaining in detail their health condition and the remedies for it. He would also journey out into the universe.

Shamans journey to the spirit world for guidance. They are considered to be healers. Many have studied long to acquire their skills, and others are the product of near-death experiences. During their NDE, they seem to have somehow acquired an expanded awareness of the workings of the universe that brings them to a level of knowing similar to a trained shaman. They often have the ability to do healings.

The use of drugs has played a role in planned OBEs throughout history. Researchers have found that 50 percent of marijuana users polled have had OBEs as compared to the 10–20 percent of nonusers polled. This is not an endorsement of drugs as a method of OBEs; there are other ways to have the experience while keeping a clear head.

Out-of-Body Experience Induction

Altered states of consciousness such as hypnosis and meditation, can be used to help induce OBEs. The suggestions for an OBE are given after the subject has been counted down into a deep state of hypnosis. Here is an example of suggestions that could be given by a facilitator to a highly hypnotized subject to guide them through an OBE.

1. You will begin to feel yourself floating upward toward the ceiling. You can look around and down on the room. As you continue to drift upward, you find yourself above the roof of where your body is located.
2. As you continue to float, you will begin to look down on the area. You can see the houses and streets as they grow smaller and smaller as you drift upward into the sky. You will see the entire landscape for miles around.
3. You now find yourself floating in the clouds. As you float out into space, you can see the whole world below. Enjoy this incredible view for a few moments.
4. Now you may begin your return journey to earth. Slowly drift downward over the town, over the roof, back into the room, and down into your body.
5. In a moment, you will come back to full consciousness feeling relaxed, positive, and amazed at your out-of-body experience.

Of course, you don't need a facilitator to do this; you can do it on your own. You can try this script or write one, memorize it, and give yourself the suggestions after you have counted yourself down from five to zero. You can travel anywhere you want, just as you can in a lucid dream.

Remote Viewing

Some people have natural mental abilities to remote view that they may not even know about. Once an individual becomes aware that he has the right abilities, he can be trained to use them for remote viewing. A remote viewer is actually projecting himself to a different location and may be an observer or, like Cayce, actually feel physical sensations, such as temperature or sound.

FACT

Sara has always had a natural ability to fly in her mind. She learned at an early age that she could actually go to places and experience the physical sensation of being there. She has remotely gone to libraries and read and researched the information in books found there.

In summary, OBEs can be experienced in several different ways, including through lucid dreaming. They can be experienced through DILDs and WILDs. They can also be experienced in altered states of consciousness, such as meditation or hypnosis.

Near-Death Experiences

It is not uncommon to have an OBE during a near death experience (NDE). Dr. Raymond Moody, in his book *Life After Life*, published in 1975, brought the phenomenon of NDEs to the general public. He found that people who had died and then came back to life reported that they were aware of OBEs during the time they were clinically dead. While they were having their NDE, many of the individuals found themselves observing their bodies from above with the realization that they were dead. Other experiences included a pain-free, peaceful feeling, passing through a dark tunnel toward a light at the end, being accompanied by guides or deceased family members, and going through some kind of life review before returning to their bodies.

For many, the experiences were nonjudgmental, and they returned with an understanding of what life may be like on the Other Side. Near-death survivors often seem to have gone through some sort of a life-altering experience during their time on the Other Side. Consequently, they look at life differently and may have a hard time adjusting to the way things were before their NDE.

A Person Can Change

NDEs can happen in times of extreme stress. They can happen mentally, spiritually, or physically. When an NDE is triggered, a part or the whole of the spirit seems to separate from the physical body and drift into the spiritual world. Even if the person doesn't remember leaving her body, she can still find that the way she perceives life has changed. Once a person has experienced an NDE, OBEs seem to come easier. It may be hard for her to feel "grounded," as she knows what it's like to "float." Some people never fully adjust to a NDE experience.

When someone goes through an NDE, her mind processes differently than before. She may not notice the difference in herself because she believes that she is thinking the same way she always did. The people around her may be aware that there is something different, but may not know the reason why. What is different is the way that she experiences life through her five senses.

What happens in a NDE is that the way a person processes images in her mind has changed. She is much more sensitive than before the experience and now reacts differently to life situations. An NDE can be both a blessing because of the increased awareness and a curse because of the increased sensitivity if the individual doesn't understand that she has changed.

NDEs are one form of OBEs. Even though an individual during an NDE is usually at peace, the situation is often brought on by a trauma. The benefit of this type of experience is the insights gained. The experience has been replicated with drugs such as LSD and by breath work. It is possible that a lucid dream or altered state of conscious experience can provide the benefits of expanded consciousness from an NDE without going through the entire trauma often associated with it.

Comparisons

How do lucid dreams, OBEs, and NDEs compare with each other? First, let's look at what they have in common. All three can be OBEs, although a lucid dream may not have an OBE. In a lucid dream, you are free to do whatever you choose. Even though the feeling of flying is fairly common, you could opt to keep your feet on the ground.

Consider conscious awareness. That, of course, is one of the characteristics of a lucid dream. In many cases during an NDE, the individual has no pulse and yet he certainly reports that he does have some sort of conscious awareness while he is in that state. So is this proof that consciousness is a part of the soul and remains a part of it after physical death? At this point, there is no developed scientific device to actually measure if something like a soul leaves the body during NDEs. Still, whatever takes place, there is often a conscious memory of an experience during the time of the NDE.

How about an OBE that took place during a dream? Would you consider the experience real or was it just a dream? If you find yourself in this situation, you could always do a reality check to see if it is a dream. So if you look at the face of a clock and it appears the same, what then? This would prove to you that you were having a real OBE like astral projection, and not a dream. Just go with the experience as you would with a lucid dream, with the understanding that you have a silver thread connected to your physical body that will keep you safely tethered as you fly in spirit. When you have finished traveling, you can return to your body.

Real or Imagined?

Is this a real experience, or is the individual just imagining or hallucinating? Are they in some sort of trance or hypnotic state? There will always be skeptics when it comes to OBEs or NDEs. The reality is how it works for you. If you have had one or more OBEs or an NDE, what insights have you gained? Are the experiences something that can help you on your journey through life?

ESSENTIAL

Mary woke up suddenly, and as she rose from her bed, she became aware that she had actually stepped outside her physical body. Becoming fearful, she carefully lay back down, and the second time her physical body got up with her. Was this an OBE, or was she just dreaming? You decide. To Mary it was real.

Lucid dreams, OBEs, and NDEs all seem to have a common thread of conscious awareness while the events are taking place. OBEs within a lucid dream give the participant the opportunity to control their journey, where in an NDE the participant is just along for the ride. A "real" astral projection experience is different from an "unreal" lucid dream. Sometimes it is hard to discern what type of experience the participant is having. It really comes down to what is real for the participant.

Astral Travel During Lucid Dreams

Astral projection is the belief that an individual has a connection to a spiritual realm that transcends out into the stars. Plato maintained that man had both a physical and a spiritual body. The astral body was able to travel into the realms of the spiritual world. As many astral projection experiences occur during dreams, it is possible to intend to have a lucid dream where you are consciously aware of your astral travels. Astral projection is not limited to visiting the spiritual world and can take you anywhere, just as other OBEs.

You can experience astral travel through a DILD, a WILD, or an altered state-induced lucid dream. The first step is to decide which way you would like to have an astral-traveling lucid dream. Once you have chosen your method, set your intentions and remind yourself of them several times a day.

Depending on what method you use and your experience in lucid dreaming, it may take a few nights or sleep times to accomplish your goals. Remember to have patience, feel gratitude, breathe in from the ground and the sky at the same time, and feel it in your heart. The more you think of your intentions to have a lucid dream astral-travel experience, the more you will be preparing for positive results.

Astral projectors believe that they are tethered to their physical body by a silver thread that acts similar to the umbilical cord of an unborn child. Some people feel that an astral projection experience is like traveling through a long tunnel, similar to a birth canal.

Here are some suggestions for all three different types of lucid dream experiences:

- **For a DILD:** Just before going to sleep, suggest to yourself after taking a deep breath and exhaling slowly, "I look forward to waking up and being consciously aware that I am dreaming. I know that I can test the reality of my dream to prove to myself that it is a dream and that I am free to astral journey. I will always be consciously aware and in control. I will clearly remember my astral travel experience afterward."

- **For a WILD:** Suggest to yourself after taking a deep breath and slowly exhaling, "As I drift off into sleep, I will remain consciously aware when I enter into my lucid dream. I look forward to proving that it is a dream and then astral traveling with complete freedom, knowing that I am connected by a silver cord to my physical body. I look forward to my lucid astral-travel dream and will remember everything completely afterward."

- **For an altered-state lucid astral-travel dream trance:** Start by focusing on your breathing, relaxing your muscles, and letting your eyes go out of focus. Suggest to yourself, "As I slowly count down from five to zero, I will go deeper and deeper with each step into my altered state of focus. By the time I get to zero, I will be consciously aware that I am beginning my lucid astral-travel dream trance. I feel calm and relaxed as I count down to this wonderful lucid dream-trance experience. I know that this is a dream, and I am in control and free to travel up the silver thread that connects to my physical body as I travel out into the spiritual realms beyond. When I have returned down the thread, I will wake up fully refreshed and excited about my adventure. I will fully remember my lucid astral-travel dream."

When you wake up from your experience, record it in your dream journal. As you develop your skill at lucid dreaming, there will be no limits to the extent of your travel. Every experience will be a new adventure. Every adventure comes packed with insights that can help you travel throughout your life.

Planned Lucid Out-of-Body Dream

We have just considered astral travel during a lucid dream. You may wonder what the difference is between astral travel and an OBE. As you may recall, in an astral journey the traveler is connected by a silver thread acting like an umbilical cord from the physical body to the spirit body. An OBE is simply free flying with or without a physical form. The OBE can be as uncomplicated as just floating above a location to something more complex, like going to a specific location, as in remote viewing.

When Mary was a child, she had a recurring dream. In it, she climbed an old-fashioned staircase, each time getting to the top only to fall back down the stairs. One night she became consciously aware before the usual fall and decided she would fly back down. She did that in perfect control and never had the dream again.

The first thing, of course, is to decide what you want to accomplish with an OBE. You could always start with something simple and work your way up to traveling anywhere you want in the universe. As you progress through this book, you will learn how to set specific goals or intentions for lucid dream experiences in a variety of subjects. Think of this as OBE 101. It won't be long before you're an expert.

As always, the first step is to set clear intentions for your lucid dream OBE adventure. After you have decided, remind yourself several times a day of your intentions. Remember to have positive expectations about your upcoming experience and to be grateful in your heart. Decide how you want to induce your lucid dream state. When you are ready, follow the suggestions made in the last section, changing the words to fit your intentions.

Don't forget to do a reality test and to suggest to yourself that you will always remain consciously aware and in control, you will fully remember your lucid dream OBE afterward, and that you will record it in your dream journal. Remember to always feel gratitude that you will have a great lucid dream experience, and remain open to the insights that can come from a lucid dream OBE.

CHAPTER 8

Develop Power Mind Images
for Lucid Dreaming

Now you will learn how you create images in your mind's eye. You will determine how you create images in your mind's eye in each of the five senses: seeing, hearing, feeling, smelling, and tasting. You will discover which of these are your strongest and weakest ones. You will try an exercise that can help you develop powerful images in your mind's eye to assist you in focusing your conscious mind on having productive lucid dream experiences.

Understand How Your Mind Images

Most people have not learned to identify how and why they think differently than other people. You can learn to understand some things about yourself and others that you may never have known before. How your mind's eye processes images makes a big difference in how you go about your life. Remember that there is no one exactly like you.

ESSENTIAL

You know that your physical DNA is different than anyone else's, and so, too, is your mental DNA. Your mental DNA is the way you create images in your mind—the way your mind's eye perceives your external experiences and internal thoughts.

You are constantly experiencing your environment through your five senses. You see what is taking place, hear what is going on, feel your surroundings emotionally and by touch, taste, and smell. All of these experiences are absorbed by your unconscious mind and are replayed in your memories. Even if one of your senses has lessened, such as your hearing or smelling, you may still have vivid images through that sense in your mind's eye.

You May Communicate in a Different Way

The term "mind's eye" is a misnomer in itself. It implies how you see in your mind. Seeing is important, but so are the other four senses: hearing, feeling, smelling, and tasting. It all comes down to how you imagine or recall information. Believe it or not, we do not all imagine in the same way. Perhaps you can think back to your schooling and remember a class that really frustrated you because the teacher taught in a way that was hard for you to understand. When we are not on the same wavelength in communication with someone else, it is usually a good indication that you do not imagine in the same way.

How many times have you heard someone say, "I want you to visualize for me . . ."? It is expected that everyone can visualize to one degree or another. That is just not true. Not everyone has the mental ability to see in his mind's eye; some people are nonvisual.

QUESTION

Where do your thoughts come from?
Thoughts in your mind are mental images that are experienced through one or more of the five senses: seeing, hearing, feeling, smelling, and tasting. When you imagine, you are creating mental images based on your thoughts.

How Do You Recall Images?

A nonvisual person does not imagine or remember with picture images in his mind. There are people who do not imagine or remember sounds in their mind, either. The same is true for feeling, smelling, or tasting. This is part of mental DNA. The imagery in your mind's eye depends on the way that you imagine or recall through the combination of the five senses.

You might wonder what this has to do with lucid dreaming. It has a lot to do with it. The first thing is how you prepare for your lucid dreams. Your intentions are connected to the way you imagine, and so are reality checks. Your conscious awareness is also impacted by the way you imagine, as is the way you dream and the way you remember your dreams.

Understanding how you naturally experience images in your mind can help you develop powerful customized imagery to help you lucid dream. Remember that you are unique and one of a kind.

Visual Images

Most people have some degree of visual recall in their mind. That is why so much communication is presented in visual concepts. If you are visual, that will work for you. If you aren't visual, then it may not be easy to comprehend or achieve when you are given visual instruction or directions only. Let's see how visual you are.

If you are ready, find a comfortable spot, take a breath, and let your mind's eye respond to the following questions. You may be able to respond to all of them or maybe none of them. You may find that some create stronger mind images than others. Perhaps this exercise will help you begin to understand a little more about yourself.

For a moment, think of a place that you are or have been connected with in your life that brings up positive memories. If you have trouble thinking of one, then just make one up in your mind's eye. You can keep your eyes open or closed or try it both ways to determine how you create your strongest visual images. Take your time and let your mind focus on the images in your mind's eye.

- Can you imagine in visual pictures? If so, are they in color, sepia, or black and white? How clear are your visual images?
- Are you seeing a still picture or is it moving? Can you move back and forth between moving and still pictures?
- If you see a moving picture, can you slow it down or speed it up? Can you replay a section of the image over and over in a loop? Can you hold the image still or does it flicker?
- Can you imagine being in the visual picture? If so, can you move around in it?
- Can you watch yourself as if you were seeing a video? Can you do both, experience being in the image and watching yourself in the image? If you can, which of the images is stronger or are they both the same?

ALERT

Can you recall pages of a book in your mind's eye? Some people have what is known as photographic memory and have perfect visual recall of almost everything they have seen during their life. It is possible, if this ability is not consistently utilized, it will eventually slip away as you age.

So what did you discover about your visual self? Do you see in your mind's eye? Remember, if you are having trouble visualizing, that just means that one of your other senses has made up the difference and you will have the opportunity to discover which one is the strongest for you as you learn more about mind images.

Hearing Images

Can you imagine or hear any sounds in your mind's eye? Let's start with the positive images you thought of for the last section.

- Can you hear any sounds in that picture in your mind's eye? If so, is there more than one sound? How loud are the sounds in your mind?
- If you can experience sounds, can you move around in the image and get closer to or go further away from them?
- Can you hear conversations? If so, can you get closer to them so that you can hear every word? Can you repeat parts of the conversation so you can hear it over again?
- Can you imagine music in your mind's eye? If so, can you turn the volume up or down? Can you change the speed of the music? If there is more than one instrument or voice, can you focus in on a single part and hear that above the rest?
- Could you imagine the sound of running water in your mind's eye and get closer to it or further away from it?
- Do you hear voices in your mind speaking directly to you? These could be the voices of positive advice and guidance often understood to be guides or angels. Perhaps you have the ability to hear and repeat messages from the Other Side or the spiritual realm. You may receive psychic advice through your mind's ability to hear.

If the voices you hear in your mind are not positive and are asking you to take actions that could be harmful to yourself or others, seek immediate help by contacting a mental heath counselor in your area. This type of voice is different from a guide or angel who is there to watch over and positively guide you.

What else can you hear in your mind's eye? Remember, if you do not imagine any sounds in your mind's eye, that is okay.

Feeling Images

Your kinesthetic or feeling sense can be a very powerful sense. It actually has two different components to it. One part is tactile or touch—the way you externally experience your environment. The second part is how you emotionally experience your environment.

Think of your positive memory image from the visual section. Here are some questions to help you understand how you recall kinesthetic images in your mind's eye.

- Can you imagine feeling what the temperature is there? If so, could you imagine what the temperature would feel like at a different time of day or a different time of year? Can you feel a breeze if your memory is out of doors?
- Can you place yourself in the scene and feel the texture of items that are there, such as the ground, the floor, the clothes you are wearing, or anything else you recall or imagine in your mind's eye? What else can you imagine touching in your favorite place?
- Could you imagine putting your hand into a bucket of ice cubes and feeling it grow cold and numb? If you can, take it out and feel your hand coming back to normal, feeling warm and comfortable.
- What does it feel like emotionally to experience a positive memory of your favorite place in your mind's eye? What other feelings do you recall from your positive memory?
- Do you ever take in and experience the emotions of other people? If so, can you increase or decrease these emotions? Do you ever feel overwhelmed by the emotions of others and then continue to experience them in your mind's eye?
- Do you feel emotions in your body? If so, where? Some people get a feeling in their stomach while others may get a "buzz" or vibration in their third-eye chakra.
- When you are dreaming, are you aware of any feelings in your body? If so, how do they compare to the feelings you experience when you are awake?
- Do you feel emotions when you dream? If so, can you have the same experience when you remember them when you are awake? If you have a lucid dream, can you create emotional or physical feelings?

- Can you remember times when you may have felt a sensation or a feeling that corresponded with an experience you were having at the same time?
- When you remember an incident in your mind, can you recall the sensation and feel it like you did before? How else do you feel information in your mind's eye?

FACT

Many kinesthetic people receive psychic information through specific emotional feelings or physical sensations throughout their body. Different sensations and feelings often mean different things. Learning to recognize these kinesthetic intuitive messages can help them recognize situations or conditions that they otherwise would have dismissed or misunderstood.

Smelling Images

Can you remember any smells in your favorite place in your mind's eye? If so, what were they? Can you remember the memory of a favorite smell and experience it again as you recall it in your mind's eye? Perhaps you have a favorite relaxing smell that you can remember. If so, take a deep breath and experience your favorite smell, and let yourself feel calm and relaxed as you do.

ESSENTIAL

Remembering a favorite relaxing smell is a great way for you to disappear for a moment in your mind. Besides the pleasing experience of the smell, the process of deep breathing can help relieve stress. As you focus on breathing in the smell, you create a light positive trance state that is detuning whatever stress you may be currently experiencing.

- Can you imagine wandering through your favorite space in your mind and experiencing different smells as you go?

- Can you imagine food cooking and experience the smells in the images in your mind's eye? Can you imagine walking through a place that has many kinds of food, and as you progress, smell the different aromas that you pass by?
- Can you intensify or decrease smells in your mind's eye?
- Do you receive and remember smells that are connected to psychic knowing or to someone that has passed?
- Have you ever experienced any smells in your dreams? If so, how do they compare to waking smells? Have you ever experienced a lucid dream where you were aware of and could experience smells?

Tasting Images

Are there any tastes associated with your favorite place that you can recall and experience in your mind's eye? If so, what are they? Can you think of a food that you enjoy and imagine what it tastes like? How about a food you do not like? If you can think of one, you do not have to remember the taste. Think of one you like instead.

Here are some more questions to help you understand how you recall tastes in your mind's eye.

- Can you look at a recipe and imagine what the finished product would taste like? Can you imagine the taste of different ingredients in the recipe? If you cook and use recipes, do you change ingredients if the recipe has something in it you do not care for?
- Are there foods you avoid because you can remember what they taste like?
- Do you get certain tastes in your mouth when you are receiving psychic information?
- Some people experience a bad taste when something is wrong. Can you recall experiences when your sense of taste has helped you avoid trouble?
- Perhaps you have a taste memory, related to someone that has died, that you still experience from time to time in your mind's eye. How else has your sense of taste provided you information?

- Do you taste in your dreams? If so, how do your dream experiences compare with waking tastes? If you lucid dream, can you experience tastes and perhaps change them if you want? Can you experience dream taste memories when you recall them in your mind's eye? How else do you remember tastes?

Putting Them Together

So, how did you do? Which senses do you imagine with in your mind's eye? Are there any senses that you do not imagine or recall memories with? You may find that you have great recall in all five of your senses or you may find that your memories are limited to only one or two senses.

The goal is to have you realize that you are who you are and to understand how your mind works. Perhaps you found by answering these questions that you were trying to make your mind work in ways that were not your strongest senses. If you are nonvisual, you will remember in a different way. You may even know answers or remember information without really knowing how you actually recall it. Once you know and understand yourself, you will begin to trust what is coming through your mind's eye.

Sensory Recall

Now it's time to put all of your senses together to help you understand how you may imagine and recall in more than one sense at a time. If you are ready, take a deep breath and think back to your favorite place in your mind's eye. Can you see the images as you hear the sounds, feel the temperature, smell any smells, or taste any tastes that may be there? Take a little time to let the image form in your mind. How many different senses were you able to use to recall your memories?

Do you feel what you see in your mind's eye? It could be an emotional feeling or a touch memory. Perhaps you feel in colors, or maybe you can experience what a color feels like. You may recall sounds in color, by emotions, or by touch. You may visualize what you are hearing or perhaps feel a vibration in the sound.

Sensory Design

You may dislike certain foods by the way they look, feel in your mouth, or smell. Taste can be connected to all of the senses. Many chefs are well aware of how their presentation of food connects with the senses of their customers. A picture can evoke many different sensations from a viewer. The viewer is tapping into their sensory recall when they are looking at a picture image.

Just about all advertising is designed to evoke the senses of the intended target audience. Perhaps you can think of some ads that are designed to connect you to the product through the images in your mind's eye. Are there any other ways you can think of in which your five senses connect together when you imagine them in your mind?

Image Exercise

Now that you have an idea of how your mind works, at least as far as how you imagine in your mind, the next step is to use what works for you. Unfortunately, many people keep trying over and over again to create mind imagery that is not natural for them. The goal is to have you imagine with your strengths rather than trying to use your weaknesses. That is not saying that you will not improve your imagery in a weaker sense. You can always keep improving, but remember your strengths.

If you add gratitude and heart power to your mental images, they become even more powerful. In this case, the word "powerful" means more vivid and real. You're back to that reality check. When you doubt yourself, you are creating the reality of failure. When you have learned to trust that in some way your intentions will result in success, you will have learned the concept of being grateful for something that you have no idea how is going to become a reality. Just believe and trust that it is already becoming a reality.

Powerful Mind Images

To start building a powerful mind image, think of something or some place that you can relate to unconditional love. Why unconditional love? When there are no conditions, there are no obstacles. Many people think of their pets or small children as unconditional love. Others relate it to their faith.

If you can identify something that you are grateful for that connects to unconditional love, you are activating your heart power. When you connect your heart that is filled with unconditional love to your intentions and experience them through your senses in your mind's eye, you are creating a strong image. Add to this image the suggestion that you are grateful that your intentions are already a reality.

Dream-Induced Lucid Dream Exercise

Let's put together an exercise for a dream-induced lucid dream (DILD). First, remember to set clear intentions for your DILD. This is an exercise that you can do when you go to bed or you can feel it several times a day as reinforcement.

When you are ready, find a comfortable place, take a deep breath, and slowly exhale. Let your eyes go out of focus as you continue to breathe in and out.

Begin to relax the muscles in your body from the top of your head down to the bottom of your feet. You may feel muscles tighten up, and if you do, just relax them as you relax more as you move into a hypnagogic state.

For a moment, think of unconditional love, and imagine it through the five senses in your mind's eye. Let yourself feel gratitude for the images that you are experiencing.

If you can, step into your images and experience them in all your senses as you continue to breathe in and out, relaxing more and more. Perhaps you can see images, hear sound, feel or touch, smell or taste what you are imagining in your mind's eye. This experience may feel very real to you, and you are consciously aware of what you are imaging.

Now think of your intentions to lucid dream. Let yourself feel grateful that you will become consciously aware when you begin experiencing a dream. You will know that this really is a lucid dream because you will do a reality check to prove that it is just a dream. You are grateful for the opportunity to experience your lucid dream.

Experience the powerful images that the dream is already a reality and you will be fully aware when it is happening. You will be able to recall in your mind's eye vivid images of your lucid dream as you record them in your dream journal.

Feel and know that you will be able to change and move in your lucid dream any way you want. Feel this in your heart with gratitude.

As you drift off to sleep, look forward to being consciously aware when you are having your lucid dream. You know that the dream will be as you intended. You look forward to your lucid dream experience as you drift off into sleep.

Wake-Induced Lucid-Dream Exercise

The wake-induced lucid dream (WILD) and altered state of consciousness trance methods start with the same relaxation exercise. As you begin to enter into a relaxed hypnagogic state, here are some suggestions for a WILD.

Imagine in your mind's eye that you are and will stay consciously aware as you drift off into sleep.

Use all of your senses to help you focus in on your intention images. You may see, hear, feel, smell, or taste to help the images in your mind's eye become clearer and clearer.

Suggest to yourself that as you begin to experience a dream, you will consciously be aware of it, and you will know that it is a dream when you do a reality check.

You will be able to observe, move around, and change your lucid dream any way that you want because you know that it is a dream and not real. Feel gratitude and unconditional love as you drift further toward sleep, still staying consciously aware.

Suggest to yourself that you will have a clear memory of your lucid dream in all of your senses after it is over, and will be able to record it fully in your dream journal.

In an altered-state induction, suggest to yourself or have the facilitator suggest to you that as you count from five to zero, you will focus in on your lucid dream trance with all of your senses. Suggest that you will be consciously aware of your lucid dream and will know that it is a dream when you test its reality. You will be able to move, observe, and change your lucid dream any way you want. You will fully remember your dream in all of your senses after it is over as you record it in your dream journal. You can feel free to add to or change these suggestions to make them more suitable for you.

CHAPTER 9

Determining the Reality of the Dream

Here you will focus on how to become more consciously aware during a lucid dream. You'll understand the importance of knowing how the images in your mind's eye prove to you that you are experiencing a lucid dream through your conscious awareness as you do a reality check. You will learn how to set an anchor for a reality check while inducing an altered state of consciousness lucid-dream trance. Finally, you will investigate how to use two different views to help you gain insights from your lucid dreams.

Conscious Awareness During a Lucid Dream

You can learn to use your senses to hone in even more on your awareness. You may have found that when you imagine in your mind's eye, you can experience amazing clarity. You may have found that it isn't as easy to create or recall images, especially if you do not have a strong visual sense. When you can see it in your mind, it seems so much more real than if you can't. That can be true when you are experiencing a dream.

Are you a visual dreamer? Are your dreams so vivid that when you wake up there is a moment when you are not sure whether the dream was real or not? At that point in time the dream was in control of you rather than you being in control of the dream. You may have been slightly aware but not enough to say to yourself that this is only a dream and is not real.

Your dream journal is probably filled with dreams that you remember but were not aware at the time you dreamed them. You may have gotten lots of information from those dreams, but you did not have the opportunity to actually step inside them and take control and investigate them further. The object here is to help you become consciously aware when you are dreaming and use your senses to step consciously into the dream to take control.

Is It Real?

Many people have experiences in a normal waking state that are similar to what happens in a regular dream. We are all constantly bouncing back and forth between the past, the future, and the present in our mind's eye as we go about our day. When something triggers a powerful image in your unconscious mind, it comes flooding back to your consciousness through your mind's eye. Sometimes these images may seem so real that you do not consciously challenge what you are experiencing. When this occurs, it can be very disorienting to the person experiencing the powerful mind images.

This is what happens to someone when, without warning, she experiences a phobia attack. She begins hallucinating, seeing and experiencing images that others around her do not. When this happens, she has, in that moment, lost touch with reality. She has actually put herself in a trance that could last for a brief moment or longer, until something brings her mind back to normal reality.

Unexpected Feelings

Perhaps you can think of times when you have been suddenly engulfed by a feeling that came out of nowhere and took over your thoughts. You may have felt sudden embarrassment, guilt, fear, sadness, or happiness. Your mood probably changed and you didn't know why or what was influencing your thoughts. You may have recognized that something was taking place and consciously interrupted the images in your mind's eye to create more positive ones. You can actually give yourself a reality check on the images in your mind's eye by pausing and asking yourself what is really going on.

ALERT

It is not only important to be consciously aware when you are in a dream; it is also important to be consciously aware when you are awake. If you find yourself dealing with an unexplained emotion, ask yourself, "Where did I learn this feeling, and is it appropriate to experience it now?"

So what does this all have to do with lucid dreams? When you know that you are in or have just woken up from a dream, you can use your conscious awareness coupled with your sensory imagery to focus on the dream. If you are awake, you can put yourself back in the dream through the dream memory you recall in your mind's eye. Knowing that you are consciously aware that you are in a lucid dream opens the door for gaining insights as you progress through the dream.

Proving to Yourself the Experience Is Real

How can we develop reality checks for ourselves so that we can maintain a firm grasp of what is really taking place around us and in our minds? LaBerge found a way to prove that he was consciously aware when he was asleep. He was able to send messages with eye movements and clenched fists that proved to his observers, along with scientific backup, that he could maintain conscious awareness when he was asleep. You probably don't have the same resources to prove that you are consciously aware when you are lucid dreaming. You have to be the judge of whether or not you are consciously aware during a lucid dream.

Before you accept how your mind imagery really works, you often need to have some sort of proof. By now, you have probably begun to understand how you recall or imagine images in your mind's eye. If you can accept that your mind works the way that it naturally does, then you have proved something to yourself. Once you have proved it to yourself, you have accepted the proof as real.

Nonvisual Proof

If you are nonvisual, how do you prove to yourself that you are in a lucid dream if you do not imagine in pictures? It is harder, but it can be done if you pay attention to what you know about the dream. Nonvisual dreamers feel their dreams. They know the whole story of the dream almost as if they were getting visual images, but they still do not recall visually in their mind's eye what they experienced. It is important for a nonvisual person to trust that they know what they know even though they may not be sure exactly how they know it.

ESSENTIAL

Nonvisual people often just know their information rather than experiencing it in their other senses. They may not be able to prove what they know by traditional concepts such as seeing it in their mind's eye. It takes time to learn to trust that what you know is real.

So, if you are a nonvisual dreamer, how can you re-enter a dream? The answer is, just imagine. After all, you were able to come up with the story of the dream without picturing it. If you are willing to just imagine and let the "knowing" in your mind's eye play out in the dream, you are already reconnecting with the dream. Just lay back and consciously let the dream unfold, telling yourself, "I know this is just a dream, and I can let myself know anything about the dream that I want to know in the way that I want to know it." That is your reality test—knowing that you are experiencing a lucid dream.

Trust

It comes down to trusting that the images you are consciously aware of experiencing in your mind's eye are the right ones. When you see that things are different in your reality test, you know that you are dreaming because you can trust the images that your mind's eye is giving you. If you are non-visual, you can trust that you are dreaming because you "just know." Use senses that work the best for you. You can also experiment by creating reality tests for yourself that include the other senses of tasting, smelling, and hearing.

Remember that your mind is different than anyone else's, and you are the only one who truly knows the reality check for your dream. Your confidence starts by reminding yourself many times a day what is real. Feel gratitude in your heart and know that it is real. Trust that you will know in your mind what you need to know at the time you need to know it, and you will know how to prove to yourself that you are dreaming and can take charge as you experience a lucid dream.

Check the Reality of a DILD Experience

Knowing how you imagine in your mind's eye can go a long way in helping you prove to yourself that you are having a lucid dream. Before you enter a hypnagogic state, as you drift off into sleep, suggest to yourself that you will become consciously aware that you are dreaming. Suggest that you intend to continue sleeping as your conscious mind proves to you that you are dreaming. Suggest that you will take control of the dream, making it lucid as you continue to sleep.

ESSENTIAL

Reminder: Consciously practice your DILD intentions during the day. Suggest to yourself that you will sleep while your conscious mind stays aware and ready to prove to you that you are dreaming when you begin to dream. Use all your senses to help create powerful image intentions in your mind's eye.

Once you have established that you are dreaming, prove to yourself that it is a just a normal dream using the reality test of your choice. Experience your reality-test images clearly in your mind's eye. Look at the image a second time and look away. Know the difference if you do not picture. Hear, smell, or even taste the difference.

With your vivid mind's eye images you know that this is just a dream because you realize that the images changed when you visited them a second time. You know that in reality they would not change. You know that you are in a dream that is not real. You know that you are in charge of the images that you will experience in your mind's eye when you become aware that you are dreaming.

Things to Do with Your Dream

Once you know that the dream isn't real, see what you can do in it. Can you move about getting different views? Can you feel yourself floating or flying? Can you look around and change what you see? Everything you can do is also proving to you that you are lucid dreaming.

Be aware of how many of your different senses are providing images in your mind's eye when you are lucid dreaming. Can you see, hear, feel, taste, or smell? What else can you do with your conscious mind while the dream is taking place? Tell yourself while you are dreaming that you will recall your dream memories in clear detail when you are awake and record them in your dream journal.

FACT

Knowing how you imagine in your mind's eye will help you when you recall your lucid dream memories. If you are nonvisual, you may be surprised at how many details your knowing can produce. You may have a visual memory without actually seeing what you are recalling.

As you develop your DILD abilities, you will become more confident that what you are experiencing is conscious awareness while you are in a dream. Eventually, all of the intentions that you constantly remind yourself of will become automatic actions. The reality test will just be a natural part of entering into and proving to yourself that you are ready to experience a lucid dream. It will be part of your dream habit.

Check Awareness During a WILD Experience

When you get set to have a WILD experience, it is important that you maintain a conscious awareness when you are drifting off into sleep. The imagery in your mind's eye can play a major role in helping keep you in touch with consciousness. The key is to prepare for a WILD experience before you even get into your sleep mode. You will want your mind as free from stimulants and stress as possible. You want to have clear intentions for your WILD.

Remember the gratitude thing. When you first lay down, focus on your breathing. As you feel unconditional love in your heart, think of what you are grateful for. Include gratitude that your intentions for your WILD are already taking place. Spend a little time with your positive feelings as you imagine in your mind's eye in all of your senses what you are grateful for. If you can observe yourself, step back and watch what you are experiencing.

As you begin to enter a hypnagogic state, suggest to yourself that you are and will continue to be aware as your body relaxes and you slowly drift off into sleep. Tell yourself:

I am aware in all of my senses that I am drifting off to sleep. As I relax more and more, I will be closer to sleep and I will remain fully aware in my conscious mind through the images in my mind's eye as I drift off to sleep. I will be aware of the dream images that appear in my mind's eye when I am sleeping. I am grateful for the WILD experience that I will soon have.

Go to Sleep

Feel yourself relaxing more and more as you drift deeper into your hypnagogic state. Stay in touch with the images in your mind's eye with your conscious mind. Experience them in all of your five senses. Feel yourself drifting off to sleep and also observe the process from outside of yourself, if you can, as both a participant and as an observer. Also realize that you may or may not be able to create both views in your mind's eye, and that is okay.

As you drift deeper and deeper, stay consciously vigilant of the transition from wakefulness to sleep that you are going through. If you have set an intention for a specific type of lucid dream, keep watch for when the first images of the dream enter into your mind's eye. If you have no specific dream goal, just stay on the lookout for when the dream images start. The dream may begin as your mind drifts from thought to thought. Then something grabs hold, and into your mind's eye pops a series of images like a daydream. Be aware of these images in all of your senses.

As you recognize that you are beginning to dream, do a reality check. Did the image change when you looked at it a second time? Did you just "know" that you were experiencing a dream? Now that you know you are consciously aware that you are dreaming, take control. Know that you will remember your lucid dream in clear detail when you record it in your dream journal.

Set Clear Intentions

In an altered-state lucid dream trance, your intentions play a large role in your success rate. You are actually programming yourself or giving yourself posthypnotic suggestions to help facilitate your lucid dream. The way you imagine your intentions in your mind's eye during your waking period using your five senses will help you in your lucid dream. You are creating powerful images to help the clarity of your mind during your dream.

FACT

You can go into an altered state of consciousness whenever you want or when your schedule permits. It all depends on what your environment permits for time and space. Using an altered state to create a lucid dream trance can also help prepare you for WILD, mnemonic-induced lucid dream (MILD), and DILD experiences.

Practice your intentions by seeing them, hearing them, feeling them, smelling, and tasting them when it applies to the way you image in your mind's eye. Practice several times a day, and after you have reminded yourself that what you are observing is real, hold the images in your mind for a brief moment. Suggest to yourself that when you are lucid dreaming, you will remember the images you practiced when you were awake. All of these exercises help build confidence that you will have productive lucid dream experiences.

Intention Anchor

You can develop intention anchors for reality checks as you count down into an altered-state lucid dream. Suggest to yourself that you will touch your thumb and finger together to prove to yourself that you are in a lucid dream. Once you have entered into an altered-state lucid dream, you can continually check the reality any time you want as you touch your thumb and finger together. Here are suggestions that you can give yourself as you count yourself down from five to zero.

- When you touch your thumb and finger together, you will be very aware of the intention you have to check the realty of your lucid dream.
- You know that you will experience clear images in your mind's eye that will prove you are having an altered-state lucid dream experience.
- You know that your intention of being aware in all of your five senses is already taking place.
- You feel positive and look forward to your altered-state dream experience.

You know that when you place your thumb and finger together you will always be able to check the reality of your dream.

Experiencing Two Views of a Dream at the Same Time

Once you are aware that you are lucid dreaming, you have many options to help you explore during your dream experience. Knowing how you receive the images in your mind's eye adds to those options. Remember that you recall and create images in your mind from two different perspectives. One is experiential and one is detached. When you are in an altered state, you are not always consciously aware of your options.

When you set your intentions for your altered-state lucid dream, also suggest to yourself that you will be able to explore your lucid dream both by being in it and by observing it. That said, you might have trouble imaging both ways. If that is the case, don't worry, as you will do an excellent job in the way images are naturally formed in your mind's eye. If you don't get the two different views, suggest to yourself that you will know the two different views when you record your dream experience in your journal. The more you practice this as part of your intentions, the more you will be prepared to experience two different views in your lucid dream.

FACT

When psychics are doing readings in an altered state of consciousness, they let the information come through them. If they are not experienced, they may not realize that they can pull back and be a conscious observer. An experienced facilitator or hypnotist can help move them around in the images in their mind's eye to help them gather facts.

Observe

Let's start as a dream observer. Suggest to yourself that after you prove that you are in a lucid dream you will imagine in your mind's eye that you are watching a movie of the dream. You are the director and can change the view, move in closer, or see it from a distance. You are consciously aware that you can hear any of the sounds taking place. You can also turn the sound up or down.

You can change locations or even characters. You can change outcomes that are not in your best interest. All of the action is in vivid images, and even though this is natural for you, you are amazed at how clear the images are in your mind's eye. If you want, you can experience the whole dream from this perspective. You are in control.

Participate

Once you have proved to yourself that you can be an observer in your lucid dream, let yourself consciously step into the dream. Now the images in your mind's eye are coming to you as if it were real. Do another reality test and look at your hand or in a mirror or at the time on a watch. Use all five senses as you experience the images in your mind's eye. If you are nonvisual, feel the dream experience and know it is real.

You can be yourself or you can be any other character or person you want to be in the dream experience. You can get to experience two opposing points of view. When you look through the mind of someone else, you can experience your information in all of your senses. You can become invisible and move in and out of situations unnoticed. You can be a hero, a lover, a scientist, an artist, a musician, or a great athlete.

Take Advantage

One advantage of inducing an altered-state lucid dream trance is that you can suggest to yourself at the end of your dream that, if you want, you can go back to the same dream and replay it or continue from where you left off, whenever you want. This is a great tool if you have limited time to experience your altered state of consciousness lucid-dream trance. As part of your intentions before you start, and when you are consciously ending your lucid dream, suggest to yourself that you will begin where you want to the next time you go back into your altered state of consciousness.

Imagine how you could use this technique to write a book or learn a skill or improve in sports. The pieces are coming together for you to do just that. It all comes down to trusting and knowing that what you are experiencing through lucid dreaming is real and has value in helping you gain a perspective on your life that is unique, different, and a natural way for you to connect to the inner wisdoms that come through your dreams.

CHAPTER 10

Tools to Facilitate Lucid Dreaming

There are several lucid dreaming aids that can help facilitate and enhance your lucid dream experiences. They range from home remedies to sophisticated electronic devices. Deep breathing and visual, sound, and aroma aids may work for you. Your mind is one of the best tools that you have, and you can create guided imagery that will help you focus on drifting off into sleep, leading to lucid dreams. The goal is to make yourself aware of the different lucid dream tool options and use what works best for you.

Material for a DILD Experience

Regardless of a dream-induced lucid dream (DILD), a mnemonic-induced lucid dream (MILD), a wake-induced lucid dream (WILD), or an altered state-induced dream trance, the first tools to consider are those that you choose to help you with your reality checks. You really should have a watch or a cell phone to keep with you at all times if you don't already for reality tests. A mirror is a good idea, one small enough to take with you. If you choose this method, you should gaze into it several times a day and make note of what the background looks like.

You may have something different in mind to use for your reality test. Whatever it is, the more contact you have with it during your wake period the more you will be able to focus on it during a lucid dream. Every time you look at one of your reality-check tools, make sure you remind yourself, "I know that what I am seeing is real, and when I look away and back again, it will remain the same."

You will also want to have a note pad and/or an audio recording device so that you are always prepared to jot down or record a thought or idea regarding lucid dreaming. The more you keep the thought of lucid dreaming in your conscious mind, the more you are creating a habit of consciously being aware during dreaming. You will want to have several bedside items to help you after you have woken up from a DILD. The most important is a dream journal. If you do not write in it until later, have material there to make notes on.

Gadgets and Remedies

Depending on your sleeping conditions, you may want some sort of portable light so you will not disturb others in your sleep vicinity. You may also want to have other devices close by, such as a computer or voice recorder. You need to have a written statement near you that is your simply worded lucid dream intention, so that you can read them at least once a day as well and repeat them often to yourself in your mind. Of course, one of the greatest tools you can have is the power of gratitude in your heart. If you don't take the time to experience love in your heart, you are missing the opportunity to use your heart power.

There are many different kinds of lucid dream supplements from simple home remedies to prepared herbs. Some of the recommendations include lemon balm tea, valerian root, African dream root, and even certain foods such as chocolate. Some people play games to stimulate their minds before retiring to help them be aware when they begin to dream. Take a moment and think of times when you have had a lot of dreams in the past. Can you think of any foods that might have helped bring on your dream?

Jon became aware that certain activities seemed to stimulate his mind during the night, causing him to dream more than usual. He learned that if he read about the ocean he would experience ocean dreams after he went to sleep. He found that if he wanted to dream of the ocean, he would read about it ahead of time.

Electronic devices designed to react to rapid eye movement when dreams are experienced during the REM period of sleep are also a way to help promote lucid dreaming. These are great tools for a DILD. Besides the visual aids, there are sound aids that can be activated during REM.

Tools for a WILD Experience

Most of the material mentioned in the first section can also be used for WILDs. As a WILD occurs from a waking state, there are certain tools beyond the ones for DILDs that come into play. One is an alarm clock; one way to experience a WILD is to set an alarm to wake you up at the time you are in a state of REM. The longest REM is near the end of your sleep period.

The goal of an alarm is to wake you up while you are dreaming so that you will be aware and can consciously re-enter your dream and turn it into a lucid dream. This method is particularly helpful for those who are having trouble becoming consciously aware enough when dreaming to create a lucid dream. Take into consideration the type of alarm that you want and need to help you accomplish your lucid dreaming goals. You may need one that won't wake up others in the household.

Once you are awake, can you go right back to sleep and still be consciously aware, or do you want to stay up for a while? You will know what is best for you. If you stay up for a while, what material do you need? Will you watch TV, listen to music, have a snack, work on a computer, or read something? Do you get up and walk around or lie in bed and then go back to your dream? You'll first need to be aware of what you will need during this period of being awake before settling back into a WILD.

ALERT

If there are others in your sleep environment, make sure what you are doing is compatible with them as you prepare for a productive WILD experience. The last thing you need is someone upset with you while you are preparing to go back to dreaming.

What else do you need to go back to sleep and stay consciously aware while you are doing it? It might help to write up what you were dreaming about when you woke up. The goal is for you to be able to recall your dream by focusing on your mind's eye imagines through your five senses. Can you do this without other tools or do you need something to help you create a deeper focus on the dream as you go back to sleep? You may want to use something to help your mind focus on your dream.

Focus

Some people use sound stimulus to help them drift into sleep. It could be the sound of a radio, CD, or TV. It could be white noise or an indoor waterfall. You might want to use a certain smell such as a candle to help you focus on your dream. It might be a point of light to gaze at as you begin to focus on drifting back into sleep and your dream. You can choose the best method for you to successfully drift into a WILD.

You might want to listen to an induction to help guide you back to sleep while being consciously aware. The wording could be as simple as, "You are focusing more and more on the images of your dream. You are consciously aware as you drift into your dream. You will know it is a dream by your reality check. You are focused on your dream."

You may come up with different tools to assist you in successfully stepping into a lucid dream. Take some time to establish your intentions and try them out in your imagination. Just imagine that you are lucid dreaming. Afterward, ask yourself how it worked. Were there any problems? If so, go back and imagine fixing the problems until you experience a lucid dream in your mind.

Deep Breathing

Deep breathing is a tool that can help you enhance your mental focus. You can use deep breathing before going to sleep to help you relax and release any stress that you have taken to bed with you. Imagine breathing in gratitude and love, and as you breathe out, feel it flowing through you and back out into the universe. This type of breathing is meditative and calming and filled with heart energy. Repeat and feel your intentions as you breathe in and out.

You may want to add color to your breathing. Think of a calm, relaxing, and positive color. Can you imagine what it would feel like to breathe that color in and then out of your body? Perhaps you can touch it and feel it flowing over and around you like a warm and comfortable blanket. A positive color added to your breathing can help you focus on relaxing.

QUESTION

How can my breathing make my imagery more powerful?
As you slowly breathe in and out, repeat your intentions as you are drifting off into sleep, and suggest to yourself that your conscious mind will know when you begin to dream. The more you imagine with all of your senses, the stronger and more powerful your imagery will be.

How about including a favorite smell as you breathe in and out? Can you imagine that? How does it feel? Suggest to yourself that with each breath of fresh air filled with your favorite relaxing smell, you will feel yourself drifting more and more into sleep as you look forward to experiencing your lucid dream. There might even be a slight taste to the right smell. Perhaps as you breathe in and out, you might think of a taste that is something fresh and relaxing.

You may select some music or a sound that you can breathe in sync with. It can be an actual sound or one you imagine in your mind's eye. You can add to the sound color, smell, and even taste if you choose while you breathe in and out. Now add some heart power. Remember that the heart generates sixty times more energy than the brain.

As you breathe in and out and focus on the images in your mind's eye, include your intentions and feel positive energy flowing down through your body. Include gratitude and unconditional love. Use this before going to sleep for a DILD or a MILD or when you are going back to sleep for a WILD, and also when you are entering an altered state of consciousness trance.

Visual Aids

Some visual aids recognize when you are in REM. The DreamLight was developed by Stephen LaBerge and Darrel Dixon in the mid 1980s. It was a sleep mask electronically wired to detect when the wearer entered into REM. When REM was detected, lights in the mask would flash to alert the sleeper that they were in the middle of a dream. This method proved to stimulate the sleeper into conscious awareness that they were experiencing a dream as long as they had included the light in their intentions.

The DreamLight was replaced with the updated Nova Dreamer in 1993. The manufacture of this device was discontinued in 2004. Today, there are other devices on the market, including the REM-Dreamer. If you want to research using an electronic visual aid, you can find both new and used for sale on the Internet.

You can use a pendulum as a visual aid to help you enter into an altered state of consciousness. You could hold the pendulum and set it down when your eyes get tired or you can attach it to a hook so it can swing by itself. A circular motion is a great way to let your eyes go out of focus. You may come up with other devices to help you visually focus on lucid dreaming.

A strobe light can be used for eye fixation as you begin to enter an altered state of consciousness trance. A hypnosis disc or spiral is often used for a similar effect. When combined with deep breathing, these devices can help accelerate the time for entering into a deeper trance. You can also download spinning discs that you can view on your computer screen.

FACT

A pendulum is a small weight such as a crystal or piece of jewelry tethered onto a string or chain. When the string or chain is held between the thumb and first finger, the weight is able to swing freely. It can be used for dowsing, connecting with the unconscious mind for yes or no answers, or for eye fixation.

Sound Aids

Several sleep masks come with a sound device in them to supplement visual stimulation when the sleeper experiences REM. The REM-Dreamer has an optional sound device called the REM-Speaker. It can prerecord your voice and play it back to you when REM is detected. The message you record for yourself can be the intentions you repeat to yourself both when you are awake and when you are drifting off into sleep. You can use a short statement such as, "I am consciously aware I am dreaming."

The goal of sound devices is to help make sure that your conscious mind is engaged in the dreaming process. You should do a reality test when you hear the sound to prove to yourself that you are aware that you are dreaming. The sound and the lights coupled with a reality test can be valuable assets for helping you create a successful lucid dream. You could also record a sound or music to help your conscious mind become aware that you are in REM.

You can listen to tapes or CDs before you enter into sleep or an altered state of consciousness trance. They can be used for sound stimuli or a sound screen to help block out other sounds that might be disruptive to entering into sleep. If you have one piece of music or sound you like, suggest to yourself several times a day that when you hear it just before your sleep period, you will focus on the sound and drift off into sleep. In your suggestions, of course, include your intentions for your lucid dream.

Recordings

You could record and listen to your own induction for an altered state of consciousness lucid-dream trance. A recorded induction can be used for a MILD. These recordings can be your voice or someone else's, and you could find generic recordings for purchase that help induce a lucid dream trance. You can also record your intentions and play them several times a day. As you are not doing an induction at that time, all you need to do to is to record a brief statement of your intentions.

You could create a subliminal recording where the words are low and covered over by music or some other sound. Your unconscious mind will hear the message. You don't have to consciously listen for the words. Imagine doing a breathing exercise as you listen to music with a subliminal message, that "soon you will experience a lucid dream while you continue to be fully aware in your conscious mind." You may have other ideas for choosing sound aids to help you focus on your lucid dream.

Aromas

You already know that your sense of smell is a very important sense. A positive smell can bring you into focus. When this smell is experienced with deep breathing, the image in your mind's eye becomes clearer and more powerful. Combine gratitude and unconditional heart love along with your lucid dream intentions, and you are creating mental images that help you in your transition to your sleep state.

If your sense of smell is strong in your mind's eye, you do not need to have an actual smell to produce an aroma. All you have to do is take a breath and imagine it as you breathe in. You can pick from a vast menu in your mind. You can try out different smells mentally to see which one will produce the best results. You can experience the same smell every time, change whenever you want, or even create a combination of aromas as if you were walking through a flower garden or a food court.

Become conscious of the smells around you while you are awake. Every time you experience a pleasant odor, remind yourself that it is real; you are taking in a deep breath and relaxing. This exercise can help you reduce daily stress and can increase your awareness of your lucid dreaming goals and intentions. Once you get in the habit of taking in a breath of a favorite smell, you will find that you are relaxing more and more in all aspects of your life. Don't forget to add gratitude and unconditional love, even in times when that seems hard to find.

ESSENTIAL

Remember that you can combine aromas with images from your other senses to help you stay consciously aware of your experiences while drifting off into sleep. Always keep your intentions in your conscious mind as a part of your imagery. Those intentions should include the reality test that you will use when you become aware that you are dreaming.

Gazing into a Mirror

Mirrors can be an excellent visual aid to help induce altered states of consciousness. Looking into a mirror or objects such as a crystal ball or tea leaves is called scrying. It is an ancient art used to gather psychic information, especially relating to the future. You can use a regular mirror or one that is made from black glass. There are several varieties of black glass scrying mirrors sold over the Internet if you would like to investigate further.

FACT

Scrying is the process of looking at any object, letting your eyes go out of focus, and seeing images come into your mind's eye. Psychics often use these images to read the future or gather information about specific people or events. Nostradamus gazed into a bowl of water to gather the information for his predictions of the future.

Placement of a mirror is important when you are using it to help facilitate a transition into sleep or an altered state of consciousness. Obviously, you are not going to want to hold one in your hands or stand and look into one. If the mirror is large enough, you can attach it to the wall or the ceiling. A smaller mirror can be placed in a stand or propped up at an angle where you can gaze into it. Of course, if it is dark, you will need to consider some sort of lighting to make the mirror visible and at the same time not too bright, to keep you from drifting off to sleep.

A candle reflecting in a mirror is a great tool for an altered-state induction. Keep in mind that the candle needs to be in a safe place where it can burn itself out. There are light bulbs that can produce a similar flickering effect. A small spotlight can also be used, and there are battery-powered lights or oil lamps that can replace powered ones.

As you gaze into a mirror, let your eyes go out of focus and open to the images in your mind's eye that are connected to your lucid dream intentions. Suggest to yourself that you can use your magic mirror in a lucid dream to help you gain insights. You can see the future or visit the libraries of the universe for wisdom and guidance. Once your eyes have closed, you can keep the image of the mirror in your mind's eye as you drift off into sleep, knowing that your conscious mind will be aware when you enter REM as you prepare to experience a lucid dream.

Sensory Mind Images

The greatest asset you have to help you prepare to have a lucid dream experience is your own mind. Knowing how you experience images in your mind's eye will help you focus on the ones that are naturally stronger for you. If you try to follow a written induction or listen to a recorded one, it may or may not work for you, depending on the images used. If you do not picture in your mind, you may have trouble connecting with visual imagery. You are who you are, so why not work with your strengths rather than your weaknesses?

ESSENTIAL

Take a moment and think about which of your senses are your strongest: sight, sound, feeling, smell, or taste. Think about images that you have found to be the most powerful for you. Now imagine how these images can help you prepare for a lucid dream.

If you see in your mind's eye, you may be able to create any visual image without actually needing a tool. If you hear in your mind, then you have all of the sound you need in your imagination. If you can feel internally in emotions or externally in touch, then use your ability to help you focus.

The same goes for smell. You do not need outside stimuli if you can create the same thing in your mind's eye. You can even imagine the taste of a favorite food in your mouth to help you focus. The more you can combine your five different senses, the more powerful the images in your mind's eye will be. Doing what is natural for you is also helping you become more comfortable as you drift off into sleep.

Guided Imagery

Finally, it comes down to gathering together all your tools to help produce the guided imagery that focuses your conscious mind on your intentions for a lucid dream experience. You can create a script that you can repeat in your mind or you can write one and record it and play it as you are ready to drift off into sleep or enter an altered state of consciousness trance. Guided imagery is just that, a process of inducing a trance or altered state of consciousness.

What do you put in your script? Here is a list of suggestions.

1. Begin with deep breathing and positive feelings of gratitude and unconditional love.
2. Let your eyes go out of focus and relax your muscles.
3. Repeat your intentions for experiencing a lucid dream, including expectations of conscious awareness and a reality test to prove to yourself that you are dreaming.
4. Suggest to yourself that you will experience positive images in your mind's eye that will help you begin to drift off into sleep or an altered state of consciousness.
5. Count slowly down from five to zero, mentioning your intentions with each step, and suggest that by the time you get to zero, you will be entering into a deep relaxed sleep. Your conscious mind will be aware when you enter REM and will do a reality test at that time. Include in

your suggestions that you will imagine the dream in all of your senses, be able to make changes if you want, and be able to recall it fully when you record it in your dream journal.

You can write your script to fit your goals and the way your mind images. You can make a CD of it and listen to it as an induction to your sleep state. You can include sound, visual images, and/or aromas if you choose. You should now have all of the tools and skills for developing techniques to help you experience lucid dreams.

CHAPTER 11

Day-to-Day
Problem-Solving Techniques

In this chapter, you'll begin to start applying the techniques of lucid dreaming for specific purposes. You will learn how to solve problems when you are lucid dreaming. You will think about the types of problems you might encounter and how to define what it is you want to solve. You will learn about the importance of faith, guides, and angels, and will have a chance to try a problem-solving lucid dream exercise.

Why Lucid Dreaming Can Help Solve Problems

Lucid dreaming is an excellent way to examine situations in your life that you are having trouble with during your waking hours. Perhaps you've heard the phrase, "Sleep on it." Many people have learned to let their unconscious minds figure things out while they are sleeping, knowing that they will wake up with the right answers. This saying can be particularly true for people who have an active conscious mind.

ESSENTIAL

If you have an active conscious mind, it may be hard for you to shut it off. If that is the case, don't even try. Breathe in and out and feel gratitude as you release your worries to the universe rather than consciously wrestling with them.

Many people with active conscious minds often have a tendency to overthink things. When this happens, they have stopped listening to their intuition and have confused themselves with too many options and what-ifs. It is during sleep that the unconscious mind can work things out without the conscious mind's interference. As a result, a clearer picture often emerges when the person wakes up.

Get a Different View

Imagine what it would be like to have the wisest counsel in the universe available to you when you need help weighing a problem or a decision. The fact is that you do, in your lucid dreams. In a lucid dream you are free to look at a situation from every angle, every side, and with input from a vast resource of experts.

That is probably the best reason for using lucid dreams to help solve problems. A lucid dream is a place in your mind where you can bring in your conscious awareness to work and play with your unconscious mind without the intellectual chatter you constantly have to deal with when you are awake. In your dream there are no ifs, ands, or buts. The dream is or can be a blank slate where you are free to consider everything from every angle.

Take Control

Does this concept sound too good to be true? Remember that it may take a little time to develop trust in what you can do in a lucid dream. When you begin to find that confidence, you will have a new tool to help you in many aspects of your life. For lucid dreaming to be effective, clear intentions for the dream need to be set just before going to sleep.

FACT

Joyce, a marketing consultant, learned that when she was beginning to develop an advertising line for a new product, she should just sleep on it. This method worked well for her throughout her career. She would always wake up the next morning with all kinds of promising ideas and was responsible for the brand names of many well-known products.

Once you prove to yourself using a reality test that you are in a dream, you are free to take control. You know that it is only a dream and therefore not real. You know that you are free to be active or to be an observer. You can examine how other people think or try out different solutions or resolutions and weigh the results. You are in charge of your own limitations in a lucid dream.

Types of Problems You May Encounter

Some day-to-day situations are simple things that can be resolved in a relatively short time. Other problems are more complex, may take more time, and perhaps several lucid dreams to work them out. Therefore, there are short- and long-range reasons for using lucid dreams to solve day-to-day problems.

Basically, we deal with two types of problems in our lives. There are the ones we create for ourselves and the ones others create for us. Most people deal with some sort of issue on a daily basis. For many people, the issues in their lives add up to stress. Stress itself can prevent you from being able to find resolutions to the issues being faced.

What Are Your Intentions?

Intention is a big and important word. Not only do you need to set clear intentions for lucid dreaming to help you deal with a problem, it really comes down to what your intentions were in the first place when the situation that created the problem first developed. Is that confusing? When you consider how you will address a problem, ask yourself, "What were my intentions?" Are you looking for self-satisfaction or a resolution for the greater good of all involved?

ALERT

If you are a perfectionist, you will never be able to find perfection. There is always something wrong, and it is often hard to see what is right. Lucid dreaming can help you get an unbiased look at all of the sides of the situation.

When you set your intentions to work on problems, whether you created them or someone else did, remember the power of your heart and unconditional love. If you suggest to yourself that whatever you are examining in a lucid dream be done through that heart power energy, you will be looking for the best outcome for all involved. If you begin to create a habit of having the best intentions, regardless of what you are doing during your daily routine of work and play, it may ease the stress of dealing with life's problems, big and small. Bringing intentions into your conscious reality gives you the chance to step back in your mind at any time and ask yourself, "What are my intentions here?"

What Are Their Intentions?

During a lucid dream, you can examine not only your intentions but also the intentions of other people involved. Your intentions can be and are often misunderstood by others. That is when you want to ask yourself, "What are their intentions?" Not only are these questions good during a lucid dream they are also good to ask yourself any time you want or need to while you are awake. When you do this on a consistent basis, you are creating a habit that will transfer into your conscious awareness during a lucid dream.

The goal of lucid dream problem solving is to create a neutral place where you can look for the best resolution. Altered states of consciousness lucid-dreaming trances can be very effective ways to help you begin to work on positive resolutions.

Define What You Want to Solve

Clearly defined intentions of what you want to experience in your lucid dreams is one of the major keys to having lucid dreams. Having intentions established and present in your conscious mind will make it easier to stay on track during your lucid dream. The situation may be complex and require more than one dream to provide you with the answers you are looking for. Keep your intentions simple so that it is easier for you to focus on them with your conscious mind. It may help you to write your intentions in your dream journal.

You may want to have an "overview" lucid dream so you can look at all the different aspects before you zero in on specifics. Once you have established a working plan or set of intentions for dealing with a problem while lucid dreaming, you can set daily or nightly dream goals. Once you have experienced a lucid dream, you can then set your intentions for the next one, depending on the results of the dream and what the current situation is with the problem that you want to solve. Unraveling a problem can be like untangling a little girl's hair—one strand at a time—and it can take a lot of patience.

Here is a list to help you define the problem you want to solve:

- State as simply as possible what the problem is.
- Does the problem involve just you or others, too?
- What were your intentions before and when the problem first surfaced?
- What are your intentions in resolving the problem?
- How do your intentions for solving the problem mix with your heart power and unconditional love?
- What is the first part of the problem that you would like to resolve?

As part of your intentions, always keep cause and effect in mind. How does the outcome that you are playing out in your lucid dream affect those involved in the situation? As you define what you want, consciously intend to look into the future during your lucid dream to see what impact the outcome will have on the whole of the problem. Intend to compare this with your intentions for the outcome of the situation in real life. Feel free to add your own ideas to the checklist.

Take One Situation at a Time

If the problem you are working with in your lucid dream is complicated, it may be a good idea to break it down into sections, situations, or conditions within the bigger picture. Keep the intentions as simple as possible so that the conscious mind can be totally aware of them during the lucid dream. Once you have gone through your checklist to define what you want to solve, you can zero in on the first part of the problem that you want to address. Keep in mind, first of all, that you may want to observe the whole situation in a lucid dream before you work on one aspect of it. If that is the case, set that as your lucid dream intention.

ESSENTIAL

Remember that it is important to use gratitude when you are setting your intentions. Gratitude begins with the acceptance that you will have a lucid dream that will help you resolve the problem you are working on. Coupled with heart power, intentions become even stronger.

Choose the one part of the problem you want to investigate first. Define that clearly in your intentions for the lucid dream. Here are some suggestions to help you define what you want to work on first:

1. Why do you want to look at this part first?
2. What do you want to learn?
3. What are your intentions for the outcome as you look at this piece of the problem?

It is important to have a positive mindset. When you accept that something is going to take place that is compatible with your intentions, you are creating a positive image for success in your conscious mind. When you enter a dream consciously aware, you are giving yourself many different options for working with your problem.

Clear intentions for resolving a situation related to your problem along with positive expectations can help you experience productive problem-solving lucid dreams. Positive expectations can also help reduce any stress that is connected to the problem, especially when coupled with heart power, love, and gratitude. The more you practice, the more experience you will gain, and the more confidence you will have in your ability to problem solve using lucid dreams.

Solving the Puzzle: Move the Piece Around

Here is a technique that you can use while you are experiencing a lucid dream. As you know, one of the first steps in putting a puzzle together is to spread out all the pieces. Sometimes there are lots of pieces in the puzzle that you want to assemble, and sometimes there are only a few. This can all be determined as you spread out the pieces and take a good look.

Usually, there is a picture of the completed puzzle handy that will give you an idea of what it will look like when you are done assembling it. Sometimes you will find pieces missing, and sometimes there are odd pieces that don't fit. These are all different situations you face when you are assembling the puzzle. Part of your intentions can be on how you want to put your puzzle together in your lucid dream.

As part of your dream intentions, think of suggesting to yourself how you would lay out and examine the pieces in your problem puzzle. Remember that by the time you are ready to spread the pieces out in your dream, you have already done a reality check to prove to yourself that you are dreaming. Because it is a dream, it isn't real, and you are free to examine and try out solutions without the worry of messing up the conclusions. You are in charge of your intentions and how you will work with the pieces of your problem puzzle.

You can try out a solution, and if it doesn't work, you can discard it. If there is something missing, you can create a piece of the puzzle and try it out to see how it fits. You can try out actions or conversations that you might have with others to see how they work. When you have put the puzzle together in a way that brings about a resolution, satisfying your intentions, remind yourself that you will have total recall of your dream when you wake up. When you have found a solution for that part of the problem, you are ready to work on another piece of the puzzle in your next lucid dream.

Working with Help from Your Faith, Angels, and Guides

Another concept as an option that may work for you in lucid dreaming is the concept of faith or belief. As you have already heard, intentions are a very important part of lucid dreaming. When you add belief to your intentions, you are creating even stronger and more focused images in your mind's eye.

Do you have some sort of faith or belief in something other than your own abilities? If so, how do you identify it? Is it connected to an organized religion? If so, how compatible is your faith with lucid dreaming? Hopefully, if you have a faith, it can work in harmony with your lucid dreams.

Who or What Goes with You?

Do you believe that there is some type of being or force that accompanies you in your life journey? It may be with you all the time or on occasions when you need it. If you believe there is something with you, how do you know? Can you see it, hear it, feel it, smell it, or get a taste of it?

Do you consider this presence to be an angel, a guide, or a connection to the universe or God? Perhaps it's an animal that has crossed over to the Other Side that still has a connection to you. Maybe you have something else that you feel watches over you on your life's journey. If so, can you identify what this energy is?

Trust and Believe

You do not have to know exactly what is with you to believe that there is something with you. Just believing can give you a sense of support. Just imagine what it would be like to have a team with you constantly to help solve problems and bring about miracles in your life and the lives of others. Whether you believe or not, in your lucid dreams you can have the help of anything you choose. If you want, you can include your belief when you are setting your intentions.

FACT

There is nothing like the feeling of gratitude that you have help when it comes to solving a problem. Knowing that you do not have to go it alone can also help in dealing with stress. Think of the words "trust and believe." Even if you can't define what you are trusting and believing in, consider them in your intentions.

When you define your intentions for your problem-solving lucid dream, include gratitude for your faith, your guides, your angels, or whatever is in your dream to help support you and guide you in resolving the problem. Feel this gratitude in your heart. Feel the love your team has to offer you. Be grateful that your team will help bring about the best resolution for all involved. Be grateful that you will wake up at the end of your lucid dream with total recall of the dream and the resolutions your team helped bring about.

Continue Positive Feelings When You Are Awake

Another benefit of lucid dream problem solving is that you can set your intentions to wake up feeling positive about what you examined during the dream. It starts by reminding your conscious mind when you are setting your intentions that you are grateful and that you will wake up after your lucid dream with a full memory of the dream, feeling positive about the results. Feeling that intention in your heart as you are suggesting it to yourself creates a positive expectation from the beginning.

You can also create an anchor for the way you feel when you wake up from your problem-solving lucid dream. As you enjoy your positive feeling, put a thumb and first finger together and suggest to yourself that you will experience this positive emotion every time you repeat the action. Try it out a couple of times when you create the anchor to experience the feeling. As you try your anchor, feel gratitude for your lucid dream experience.

FACT

Positive feelings are, after all, an emotional experience. You may be able to combine your feelings with positive visuals, pleasing sounds, relaxing smells, and pleasant tastes to create powerful positive imagery in your mind's eye. Don't forget to be grateful as you experience these feelings in your heart.

When you include your faith or belief with gratitude for the help that they provide in your positive feelings, you create even more options for re-experiencing what you received from your lucid dream. Consciously use your anchor several times a day and feel the positive feeling you experienced when you woke up. At that time, remind yourself that you intend to feel this every time you use your anchor. The more you practice, the easier it will be to bring back these positive feelings.

Lucid Dream Problem-Solving Exercise

Here is an exercise script that you can adapt for lucid dream problem solving. You can put in the wording that works best for you and record it and play it back to yourself, either before going to sleep at night or as a self-induced altered state of consciousness lucid-dream trance any time of the day or night. If you are using the altered-state approach and have a certain period of time, you can include in your intentions that you will wake up, coming back to the surface of your conscious mind with total recall of your dream experience. If your tape is long enough, you can also suggest to yourself at the proper time that you will now finish your lucid dream and fully wake up when you count yourself from zero back up to five.

Set Your Intentions

Remind yourself several times a day of what they are. Be grateful that you will have a lucid dream experience that will provide the right resolution to your problem. Remember to remind yourself of the reality check you will do when you are aware that you are dreaming. This exercise is written with the premise that you can record it and listen to it as you make the transition into sleep.

Relax and Breathe

Make yourself comfortable in the position you will use for your lucid dream. For a moment, take a deep breath, one that is comfortable for you, and slowly exhale. As you continue to breathe in and out, let your eyes go out of focus. If your eyes are closed, you may feel them looking slightly upward under your eyelids. You may feel the muscles in your body relaxing as you continue to breathe in and out.

Feel Gratitude

Let your gratitude combine with unconditional love as the energy flows through your heart. Open your mind's eye to positive images in all of your five senses connected to your heart energy, gratitude, and unconditional love as you focus on your lucid dream intentions. Be grateful that you will consciously become aware when you begin to dream and will do a reality test to prove to yourself that you are in a dream.

Include Your Team

Feel gratitude that your team of faith, guides, and angels are there to help guide you through your lucid dream as you work on the resolutions to your problem. As you slowly begin to drift off into sleep, suggest to yourself that your conscious mind will stay fully aware, and you will be able to totally recall your lucid dream experience after you have woken up.

The Countdown

As you start your countdown, you will continually remind yourself of your lucid dream intentions. Let yourself feel peace, love, and gratitude as you count down from five to zero, each step of the way drifting further and further into sleep. This will help you stay consciously aware as you make the transition.

5. You are beginning to drift off as you relax more and more while your conscious mind will stay fully aware. You are very aware of your dream intentions. If you need or want to at any time, you can always wake up out of your dream feeling positive and rested.

4. You are relaxing more and more as you continue to drift into your sleep state. When you reach zero, you will begin to dream, experiencing it through all five of your senses. You will be consciously aware that you are dreaming.

3. Deeper and deeper to sleep you drift while you are still focused with your conscious mind that will know when you are dreaming. When you are aware that you are dreaming, you will do a reality test like looking at your hand or at a clock or a watch. When you know you are dreaming, you are free to explore your lucid dream with the help of your guides or whatever travels with you.

2. You are getting closer to your dream state. You are aware and focused on your lucid dream intentions. The more you drift into sleep, the more your conscious mind is aware and ready to participate in your lucid dream. You look forward to this problem-solving experience.

1. By the next number, you will be aware that you are dreaming. You will test the dream's reality and prove to yourself that it is a dream. You know that once you are in the dream, you can change it any way you want. Your team is there, waiting to guide you.

0. You are now dreaming. Test the dream's reality. Now you know it is a dream and you are free to do anything you want. Let yourself focus on the problem you want to solve. Let your team help guide you to the right resolutions or answers for the problem situation. You may hear a voice guiding you or feel a presence with you.

Let yourself be guided to examine all angles and sides of the problem. You can experience it from many different views. Weigh all the outcomes while feeling at peace. When you are ready or when you suggest it to yourself on a recording, come slowly back to being fully awake.

0. You are now coming back to the surface of your mind feeling positive about your lucid dream experience.
1. Coming back more and more. You will have total recall of your lucid dream when you wake up.
2. You are waking up more and more.
3. You will soon be fully awake, feeling positive.
4. On the next number you will be fully awake, feeling positive about your problem-solving lucid dream, and will remember it fully.
5. You are fully awake and feeling very positive about your lucid-dream experience as you fully recall it for your dream journal.

If you record this for yourself, change the word "You" to "I." You can either suggest to yourself that you will wake up and fully remember, or you can record the count up to help you wake up. This exercise is particularly useful for a short altered state of consciousness lucid dream where you do not have a full night's worth of sleep to work with.

CHAPTER 12

Enhance Creativity

Now you will learn to use your lucid dreams to enhance your creativity. You will have a chance to feel what it is like to be a musical performer or an incredible dancer in your lucid dreams, or study with the great artists of all time. You will see how you can write a novel or beautiful poetry. You will learn how you can create anything you want in a lucid dream and have a chance to try out a lucid dream creativity exercise.

Practice in Your Mind

One of the benefits of mastering lucid dreaming is the opportunity to be productive while you are sleeping. Once you begin to lucid dream, you are in charge, and you can use the dream to try things out. You could develop a skill. Even if you are just a beginner, in a lucid dream you can experience what it is like to be an expert.

You can create practice goals for anything you want to practice in your lucid dreams. The more specific and clear you make your practice intentions, the better the chance for a successful experience. You can consciously change a dream any way you want, but it could certainly be more productive to define what you want to experience in a lucid dream before you drift off to sleep. Take a little time to define what your practice goals might be.

FACT

Just as most productive practices are organized with specific objectives in mind, so should a lucid-dream practice be. It makes no difference whether it's a musical skill or a sport or a foreign language; the more organized you are, the more productive your lucid dream practice will be.

Here are some questions you may want to ask yourself as you create your practice intentions:

- **What do I want to practice in my dreams?** If you have more than one objective, choose the one that you want to practice first. You may want to pick something that you are familiar with and you have some ability at. In your lucid dream, using a skill you know will help make it easer to focus on your goals.
- **Why do I want to practice this objective?** If you can define why or what motivates you to practice and improve your chosen objective, it can help motivate your heart to become involved in feeling your purpose. That helps intensify your intentions. Remember, the heart puts out sixty times the energy of the brain, so feel it as you think about it.

- **What good will it do others when I improve my skills?** This question is also connected to your goal motivations. When you can define how your improvement may help positively influence others, it helps add to the purpose of practicing.
- **What part of my chosen goal do I want to practice in my lucid dream?** If you break your practice down into segments, you can focus in on parts that may need more improving than others.
- **How do I want the practice session to go?** If you define how you want the lucid dream practice session to go, you may find that by prioritizing you are actually creating an efficient lucid dream. For instance, start by practicing something familiar to you. Next, review something you have recently practiced and then proceed to something new or more difficult. Always end the session with something easy that is fun so you will look forward to your next lucid-dream practice session.

Write down your practice intentions in your dream journal. Make them simple enough so that you can memorize them. Repeat them to yourself several times a day to help keep your intentions in your conscious awareness. Remember to use gratitude for the opportunity to practice your chosen objective during a lucid dream.

Work on Your Musical Skills

Perhaps you are already an accomplished musician, or maybe you are trying to work up enough courage to sing with a karaoke machine. It makes no difference what your abilities are; lucid-dream musical practice can help you improve and perhaps achieve your musical intentions.

In lucid dreaming there is no such thing as "not good enough." You can be as good as you desire and even a legend in your own dreams. You can start by setting an intention to get some coaching from one of your favorite stars. Just intend or desire that they will be in your dream to patiently show you how it's done. Be grateful that you are getting so much help and encouragement.

Try blending your voice with theirs as you sing your favorite karaoke song together. You can pick where you want to practice. No one else has to be there as you perfect your performance. As you practice the song over and over, experience yourself assuming more of the performance as your star friend fades into the background while still encouraging your performance. Feel your confidence growing with each run-through of your song.

Face an Audience

When you are ready, pick where and when you will perform for your admiring friends and family. Feel the excitement as you step on stage and give a flawless performance. Experience the accolades of the audience as you do an encore. You could bring on your star friend to do a duet, complete with live backup band. Let your mind's eye take in this performance through all of your five senses: seeing, hearing, feeling, smelling, and tasting, while suggesting to yourself that you will fully remember your lucid dream when you wake up.

ALERT

Regardless of your musical ability, a lucid-dream musical practice schedule can help you develop and improve your musical skills. In music, practicing is part of a goal intention. The more you look forward to lucid dream practicing, the more the intention stays in your conscious awareness.

If you have performance anxiety, you can help yourself get over it in your lucid dreams. First, think of where you are the most comfortable performing. Second, what are your performance fears? Set your intentions to work through and resolve your fears in a friendly place where you feel comfortable. Now let yourself have the lucid dream experience, free from anxiety.

Advanced Study

If you are more musically advanced, you can choose a teacher that you have always admired and wanted to study with. You can work on specific passages in your music, doing them slowly and gradually increasing speed as you feel yourself responding with precision and accuracy. You can intend that you will remember how to play the same way when you are back in a waking state and as you perform the exercise in the future. You can work on memorizing a selection or adding expression.

If you are a jazz musician, you can choose to work on improvisation or playing by ear or taking performance risks to see how they work out. If you want, you can play with the best symphony orchestra known or have a meeting with the best musical minds, living or dead. You can also work on your musical composition, creating and then hearing the music that came to you in your mind's eye.

Dance in Your Dreams

Lucid dreaming can help you improve your ability to dance, no matter what your level of skill or the type of dancing you do or want to learn. In your lucid dream, you are in control and can dance the night away at a club or in a ballet. Even if you have a physical handicap, you can dance in your dreams, free from obstacles that may keep you off the dance floor during waking time.

Many serious dancers are already used to running through performances in their mind. They visualize themselves by experiencing their moves and by watching their performances in their mind's eye. By mental practicing, they develop muscle memory that will help them when they are actually performing their dance routine on stage. Lucid dream dancing can provide another way for them to develop their skills.

Lucid dreaming can also provide the opportunity for dancers to perform in front of live audiences while they sleep. They can be helped by the best teachers and coaches and perform with the best dancers. They can dance on the world's stages. There are no dance limitations during a lucid dream experience.

Intentions

Perhaps you want to learn a certain dance step or practice your moves. Set lucid dream intentions and repeat them often during the day to keep your conscious mind aware of your goals. Feel gratitude and joy about your opportunity to dance in your dreams. Choose the reality test you want to use when you become consciously aware that you are dreaming. Remind yourself of what is real during the day to help reinforce your awareness of the proof that you are dreaming when you are asleep.

However you would like to experience dancing in a lucid dream, you will want to set clear intentions. You may not have as intense a desire to dance or do other artistic activities in your dreams as others do. This may determine how serious you are as you develop your intentions. Intentions can help you prepare to take an action when you become consciously aware that you are dreaming.

ESSENTIAL

You may be very anxious to put your new knowledge of lucid dreaming to work. Remember, it may take time and patience to develop your lucid dreaming technique. You may find the altered state of consciousness lucid-dream trance to be a good way to begin.

If you are serious about your dancing, you may want to use a more intense lucid dream technique such as wake-induced lucid dreaming (WILD) or try an altered state of consciousness lucid-dream trance. Both of these methods can be used during the day or for shorter sleep periods and may provide more consistent lucid dream experiences than a dream-induced lucid dream (DILD). As you progress through this book and develop your lucid dreaming skills, you will determine what technique is right for you.

Create Beautiful Paintings and Sculptures

You can create art of all kinds while you sleep. It doesn't matter what your actual artistic skills are. In your lucid dream, you are in control, and you can be whatever you want to be.

You can experience what it is like to be a great painter by becoming the painter in a lucid dream. You can see how he sees colors and shadows. You can feel what it is like to hold a brush in your hand and actually paint as the artist does. You can be the artist and remember the muscle movements and the mental images the artist experienced when you wake up from your lucid dream.

Here are some suggestions to help you have a productive artistic lucid dream experience:

1. Determine what your intentions are for your artistic dream experience. Make them simple and easy to remind yourself of your goals during waking hours.
2. Research the style you want to experience. Learn about the history and which artists best represented that style.
3. Consciously imagine during the day what it was like to live in that period. By imagining, you are reinforcing your intentions and keeping your conscious mind primed for when you dream.
4. Let yourself feel excitement and gratitude as you anticipate your lucid dream experience. This is just a reminder of the Law of Attraction.
5. As you drift off to sleep, keep your intentions in your conscious mind suggesting that you will experience what they are as you prove to yourself that you have control of your dream.

If sculpture is your interest, you can help develop your awareness of three-dimensional form through lucid dreaming. Imagine that you could look at a solid piece of marble, wood, or clay and be able to see a shape already there. All you need to do is take away the excess material and the sculpture springs to life. You can mold, shape, and carve through the eyes of great sculptors from any time period. Suggest to yourself as part of your intentions that you will be able to recall what it feels like to be a great painter or sculptor when you actually paint or sculpt.

One of the greatest benefits to lucid dreaming is that you can have a realistic experience while you dream. Your memory of your dream can be just as vivid as a memory of an actual experience. You can make lucid dream experiences as real as you want them to be.

Write a Novel, Short Story, or Poetry

You can be a writer in your lucid dreams, and you can recall what you have written after you wake up. This may be the perfect time to honor the writer in your soul.

Here are some questions to help you set your intentions to investigate and develop your writing talents:

- **Do you write now?** If so, how would you like to improve your writing? Think of what your abilities are, perhaps what other people tell you about your writing, and the areas that you feel are blocked or need a little extra push.
- **What do you want to write?** Do you want to write a novel, a short story, or poetry? What is your secret desire? Your answers will help you set your intentions for your lucid dream writing. Create a section for your writing project in your dream journal.
- **Why do you want to write?** Is there a reason that you feel you want to write? What good will a writing project do you? What good will your writing do for others? If you have a purpose for writing and feel in your heart that you should write, you are creating powerful intentions to help keep the project in your conscious mind.
- **How, when, and where will you write?** Will you actually write in longhand or on computer? Do you have a time every day that you can write without interruption? Where will you write?
- **How will you recall your lucid writing dreams?** It is important to suggest to yourself that you will recall your lucid dream writing experiences after you wake up. It is also important that you have some writing implements available when you wake up that you can make notes on at that moment.

ALERT

Set a realistic goal. A novel may seem impossible to write because of time and size. Start with something smaller. To be successful, some sort of a consistent daily routine needs to be established, not only in your lucid dream writing but also in your waking state writing.

The world you live in as well as your dream and writing worlds needs to be taken into consideration when you set your goals. It's important to have people connected to you supporting you rather than trying to sabotage you.

Some people (and pets, for that matter) feel that when you are writing, you are taking time away from them. Sharing what you experience in your lucid dream writing as well as daytime writing may help others, if they are so inclined, to stay connected to you while you work toward your goals.

Create Anything You Want

You have the ability in your lucid dreams to create anything you desire. So, do you know what you want to create? Believe it or not, a lot of people don't even try because the thought of creating something can seem overwhelming. Here are some questions to help you consider how you can set your intentions to use lucid dreaming to help you define and reach your creative goals.

- If you had no limitations to stop you, what would you create in your life that gives you the greatest positive feelings of doing something that will be good for others? (Remember, there are no obstacles in the way in your thoughts and dreams.) Write that down in your dream journal.
- Can you imagine watching your creation become a reality? Create an image of your thought in your mind's eye through your five senses as it goes from an idea to a finished creation.
- Can you feel in your mind the joy of your creation doing good for others? It might be something that inspires them, heals them, or provides some other benefits. Imagine feeling the love that comes back to you as others benefit from your creation.

Imagine your heart feeling gratitude and love for the success of your creation. Thank your belief for making your creation a reality. Now intend that you will experience how you will create what you desire during your lucid dream. Experience your creative dream intentions several times a day, reminding yourself that when you are consciously aware that you are dreaming, you will have all the resources you need to create what you desire in your lucid dream.

Paradigms

Self-doubt is one of the biggest obstacles that stop people from reaching for their creative dreams. They are afraid that if they try, they will fail. It is hard to change the thoughts that have held them back, often for a good part of their lives. These thoughts are known as negative paradigms.

QUESTION

What is a paradigm?
A paradigm is a thought that can turn into a series of thoughts that all have the same meaning. If someone is used to thinking that she will fail, she will continue to set herself up for failure until she changes her thought patterns to succeed.

Creative lucid dreaming is a great way to change old negative paradigms. In your dream, there are no obstacles. You can learn to feel what it is like to successfully create. You can recall this feeling after your lucid dream is over to help propel you forward to finishing your dream creation in reality.

Lucid Dream Creativity Exercise

Here is a lucid dream creativity exercise you can try. You can use part of this to help set your intentions for a DILD or you can use most or all of the exercise for the other lucid dreaming techniques. You may find that using an altered-state lucid dream trance on a regular basis will be an effective way to assist you with your creativity goals.

First, define your goals or intentions for using lucid dreams to help you with your creativity. Set your intentions down in your dream journal. Keep them simple and focused on the goal of each session. Your last lucid dream session will help you determine your next lucid dream intentions.

You may want to create a goal chart with the overall goal on top and the stepping stone goals below, leading upward to the top goal. It is a great way to help you define what you want to work on next. It is also a way to chart your progress and help keep you on track. You may have defined in your mind a clear path to the top or you may just want to focus on one step at a time.

ESSENTIAL

Create simple goals to start with. You may want to make a schedule of your intentions in your dream journal. Have an overall goal that may or may not have a completion date as well as daily and weekly goals. Make regular adjustments of your goals as needed.

Suggest to Yourself

Repeat your intentions to yourself several times a day. Remember to feel excitement and gratitude in your heart as you consciously think of your intentions. Suggest to yourself that when you are ready to drift off into sleep, either during the day or at night, you will remain consciously aware of your goals and will know when you are dreaming. Following is an exercise you can try during the day or at night. You can suggest this to yourself or make a recording and play it to yourself.

When you are ready, make yourself comfortable in the position you would like to experience this exercise. Take a comfortable deep breath and slowly exhale. Let your eyes go out of focus as you continue your relaxing breathing. Suggest to yourself that you will remain consciously aware as you drift off into sleep or an altered-state lucid dream trance. Let yourself feel gratitude and positive feelings in your heart as you look forward to your creative lucid dream.

Count Down

Suggest to yourself that you will realize when you begin to dream and will prove to yourself that you are dreaming with the reality test you have chosen to use. As you drift deeper and deeper, remind yourself of your lucid dream intentions. Begin to count yourself down from five to zero.

5. You are looking forward to your creative lucid dream. You are aware of your intentions in all five of your senses as you drift closer and closer to your lucid dream state.
4. You relax more and more with each count, staying fully aware with your conscious mind as you drift deeper and deeper. You look forward to your creative experience.

3. You are halfway there. You are relaxing more and more. You remind yourself of your intentions and the reality test you will use.
2. You are getting closer and closer to your lucid dream. You feel positive and look forward to your creative experience.
1. Suggest to yourself that you will fully recall your lucid dream creative experiences when you wake up. On the next count, you will become consciously aware that you have drifted off into sleep and are ready to begin to dream.
0. You are now ready to consciously become aware that you are dreaming. When this happens, test your dream with a reality check to prove that you are dreaming. Once you know this is a dream, you are ready to begin to create.

You are now free to work on your creative goals. You may experience your dream in all five of your senses to help produce vivid images in your mind's eye while you are dreaming. There are no limitations. You are free to be as creative as you desire. You will recall your creativity fully when you wake up from your lucid dream experience.

Come Back

When you are ready or it is time, you may count yourself back up to the surface of your mind or you may wake up from your lucid dream. You will remember your creative lucid dream experience fully when you make notes in your dream journal or when you actually work on the creative subject of your lucid dream. You will feel positive, rested, and relaxed after your lucid dream experience.

1. You are beginning to come out of your lucid dream state.
2. You look forward to writing in your dream journal and to actually working on your creative project.
3. You are coming back to the surface of your mind feeling rested, positive, and relaxed.
4. On the next number, you will return to full consciousness and you will fully recall your lucid dream experience.

5. You are now back to being fully awake and feeling positive and relaxed. You look forward to writing your lucid dream experience in your journal. You look forward to your next lucid dream creative experience.

As you develop your lucid dreaming skills, you will find it getting easier and easier to reach your creative goals. You have to be willing to take the time and have the patience to achieve your desires. Lucid dreaming can go a long way toward getting you there.

CHAPTER 13

Develop a Skill
or Athletic Ability

In this chapter, you will learn how to use lucid dreams to develop your athletic abilities or any skill you want. You will consider the advantages of getting two views of the same mental scene. You can decide how to set up a lucid dream practice or game schedule. You will have the opportunity to discover the power of using suggestions before and after your lucid dream and have a chance to try doing a self-hypnosis suggestion exercise.

Lucid Dream to Enhance Your Athletic Ability

You may not think that you can train athletically while you sleep, but you can through lucid dreaming. No, you aren't going to work up a sweat dreaming that you ran a marathon. You can, however, have a marathon experience that can help you when you actually run a marathon. You can create and experience virtual reality in your mind in a lucid dream.

Racecar drivers use video simulators or games to help improve their racing skills. They can choose the track that they are scheduled to race at to get familiar with the turns and straightaways. In fact, drivers have actually won at tracks they have never raced, partly because of video practice. Lucid dreaming can provide the same experience, only more real.

Visualization

In most sports, athletes use visualization to help them prepare for an event or a specific move or action as a part of their competition. A skier will often walk a course before the race, memorizing all the gates in the course. Before she swishes down the mountainside, she will often go over the course again in her mind, imagining what it feels like to actually be skiing it.

FACT

A good athlete often has the ability to imagine experiencing his sport as well as being able to dissociate and watch himself competing. He is even able to split the image in his mind so that they can experience and watch at the same time.

Golf is another example of a sport that uses a lot of visualization. When putting, a golfer will look at the undulation of the green between the ball and the hole and then picture in his mind the ball breaking perfectly as if it was following some sort of a beam, guiding it into the cup. Interestingly enough, even when a golfer makes a poor shot, he will correct it right afterward, visualizing the same shot as if it were perfect. This helps change the image memory in his mind of the poor shot.

One of the benefits of using lucid dreams to enhance athletic ability is that you are building muscle memory in your dream. What is muscle memory? Muscle memory is achieved when a physical action is practiced over and over until it becomes absorbed by the unconscious mind, just the same as a visual memory. The goal is to train your muscles to move correctly without consciously thinking about them moving.

In the Zone

A good athlete has the ability to put himself in the "zone." The zone is a form of trance where time and distance become distorted. A basketball player can bring the basket in her mind's eye from thirty feet away to within arm's reach. The baseball player can slow a ninety-mile-an-hour pitch so that he can make contact with his bat. Speed racers break time down into tenths and hundredths of a second.

Lucid dreams can help you experience what it is like to be in the zone. You can practice moves over and over again and recall how it feels to build muscle memory. You can also feel what it is like to compete in front of a large crowd or on a championship level. Lucid dreaming can be a powerful tool to help you athletically advance in your sport.

Big Picture–Little Picture

A hologram is an image that has more than one view. Perhaps you have seen holograms projected by laser beams that appear to be three-dimensional. Some credit cards have a hologram on them. These are usually pictures that have more than one image in them, and when they are viewed from a different angle, the second image emerges.

In order to get the most out of your abilities, you need to understand how your mind processes so that you can develop your strengths and diminish your weaknesses. In a lucid dream, you may be able to experience reality images as if they were actually happening at that time even though you may not recall your dream the same way as you experienced it.

Types of Image Recall

If you are nonvisual, you will remember events in your life differently than people who are visual. Your memory picture of a lucid dream will be the same way you recall other events. You may know what you saw without being able to see it again. If you do not see in your mind's eye, you will probably not be able to use the big picture-little picture technique to help you develop your skills. Don't worry; lucid dreams can help you experience the practice and competition as if it was a real memory of a real event.

When you set your intentions to develop an athletic ability or any other skill, you need to remember how you recall images in your mind's eye. If you are nonvisual, you may want to practice a move over and over again to help you develop muscle-memory recall of your lucid dream experience. Remember, in your lucid dream you are in control, and you can focus on what it feels like to be in the zone when things just seem to flow. You will also want to be aware when things aren't flowing well so that you make the corrections in your lucid dream. Making corrections in your dream will help you recognize and make corrections when you are actually competing.

If you are visual, you can practice or compete and watch yourself at the same time in your lucid dreams. You can also feel how you are performing and watch yourself at the same time and remember both experiences afterward. You are developing muscle memory and becoming able to intellectualize what was right and wrong with your performance. You can dream past experiences, analyze them, and then make changes, just as you can change a nightmare in a lucid dream. You will also have benefit of lucid dream recall for both competition and practice strategy.

Play a Game or Practice a Single Aspect of the Sport

There is a saying in the music business that goes something like, "How do you get to Carnegie Hall? Practice, practice, practice." Before you are ready to perform at Carnegie Hall, there are many hours of practice ahead of you.

You can practice, practice, practice in a lucid dream, and you have the opportunity to perform there anytime you wish, even before you have played a single note. You can have your athletic cake and eat it, too, in a lucid dream. You can focus on practice or on a game or you can stop the game and practice anytime you want. At the same time, every experience in your lucid dream is helping you develop your ability or skill in whatever you have chosen to dream about.

Your Sport Goals

As you prepare to use lucid dreaming to develop your athletic ability, you will want to begin to set your goals or intentions. Here are some questions you may want to ask yourself to help you define what you want to accomplish. You can use your dream journal or create one specifically for charting your progress in your chosen sport.

- **What sport do you want to focus on?** You may change your sport every season, like football in the fall, basketball in the winter, and baseball in the spring. You may be on sports teams in school or play in adult leagues that only meet for part of the year. If that is the case, you can always change at the end or beginning of a season.
- **What are your improvement goals for your sport?** Maybe you just want to have fun and relax. If that is the case, your goals may be different from someone who is a serious competitor. You may want to go as far as you can in the sport, even on to the professional level. It is important to realize that everyone will have goals that are different.
- **Why do you want to improve your athletic ability?** Will developing your ability help others in some way? If you have a good feeling in your heart about what you are doing, it will help create stronger images to help you reach your goals.
- **How will your athletic goals affect others in your life?** This is an important question. If you become immersed in your sport, both mentally and physically, how is your daily environment going to be affected? Will others try to sabotage or support you as you work toward your goals?
- **What kind of a daily lucid dreaming training schedule do you want to create?** When you set your intentions, give yourself a variety of goals to work on. Warm up first and then work on routines. Go over them several times. Always participate in some competition in your lucid dream. This helps you get ready for the real thing.

Finally, if you are on a consistent lucid dream training schedule, take a night once a week or so and play another sport in your dreams. There is a term for this in sports—cross training. It is good for your mind, and your lucid dreaming practice routine won't become stale. Just remember to include in your intentions what your goals for your lucid dream practice session are, whether it's to play a competitive game or to practice a specific part of your game.

Athletic Lucid Dream Exercise

Now that you have asked yourself some questions that can help you develop your lucid dream intentions to develop an athletic skill, it's time to set your intentions down in your journal. Remember that you are the coach, the trainer, and the athlete, all in one. You are your lucid dream manager, and expressing your intentions several times a day and before your sleep period is helping to prime your lucid dream "pump." Once you have proved to yourself that you are dreaming, you are ready to start your athletic training objectives.

ESSENTIAL

Hint. During the day, consciously think of your sport and look forward to your next practice or playing session. Take a little time to visualize, if you can, participating in your sport. Use all five of your senses. Before going to sleep or into an altered-state lucid dream trance, experience your sport in your mind's eye.

You may find that the altered state of consciousness lucid-dreaming trance will work well for you as you develop your athletic abilities. Many high-level athletes, especially those who work with a sports psychologist, are already doing something very similar as a part of their daily training routine. It is not uncommon for an athlete to use visualization or self-hypnosis to put himself into an altered state of consciousness to improve his sport's performance. Mental training is a big part of the total athletic-training process.

You can use the whole of this exercise script or part of it. You can record it, memorize it, have someone else read it to you, or make up a completely different one, whatever works best for you. You can use this exercise on a daily basis during the day for a short session of a half hour or more depending on your schedule, or you can use it just before going to sleep at night.

Remember to consciously state your intentions several times during the day and imagine them in your mind's eye. Intend that you will be consciously aware when you start to dream, that you will prove it is a dream, and that you will vividly recall your lucid dream when you wake up.

1. When you are ready, place yourself in the position in which you want to experience your lucid dream. Take a deep relaxing breath and slowly exhale as you feel gratitude in your heart.
2. Let your eyes go out of focus and your muscles relax as you repeat your intentions to yourself, imagining them in your mind's eye in all five senses.
3. Suggest to yourself that you will be consciously aware when you start to dream, experience your intentions in your lucid dream, and fully recall your lucid dream experience when you wake up afterward.
4. Count yourself slowly down from five to zero, repeating and imagining your intentions as you drift closer to your dream state. Slowly breathe in and out as you look forward to your lucid dream.
5. Suggest to yourself that your muscles will remember the athletic experiences you have in your lucid dream, just as they would from an actual practice or event. Suggest that your dream is like many hours of practice even though it is much shorter in real time.
6. As you get to zero, or sooner if you are ready, let yourself go to sleep while your conscious mind remains fully aware.

After your dream has finished, you may wake up, continue to sleep, or count yourself back to consciousness from zero to five and come back to the surface of your mind, fully aware of your surroundings and ready to recall your lucid dream.

Dream to Improve Any Skill You Want

You can use the athletic lucid dreaming technique to improve any skill you want, not just an athletic skill. All you need to do is decide what you want to improve and create your intentions. It could be for improving your cheerleading skill, for example. You can practice different aspects or you can sit in the audience and give a critique of your performance. You are in control.

You may want to improve your skills at a game such as chess. There are so many different ways you can go about improving in chess while you lucid dream. You can actually put yourself in the mind of your opponent to know what she is thinking and what her next move(s) will be. You can try different moves yourself to see how they work out. You could make the game three-dimensional as if you are playing with real characters, perhaps in a different time period.

You can work on any hobby that you want to improve through lucid dreaming. It could be game playing (like cards), a sport like rock climbing, baking, or even researching history or the genealogy of your family. You can climb any rock formation in the world, try out the most creative food recipe, or even go back and talk with your ancestors during a lucid dream. All you need to do is decide on your intentions.

People Skills

You can improve a job skill or work on a hobby using lucid dreaming. Perhaps you have a new job or want to advance in the one you have. Decide what you want to improve and imagine what you would do to complete the improvements. Once you have decided on your goals, write them down in your journal as your intentions. You can take a small aspect of your job or work on the whole of it.

ALERT

You may find that your problems at work are caused by other people, including bosses, and not by you. You can use lucid dreaming to help you get a different perspective on work-related issues with other people.

Maybe you want to improve your communication or people skills. Take a moment and list your good qualities and the qualities that you would like to improve. See them in your mind's eye and imagine how you would perceive yourself once you have reached your goal. When you create your intentions for your lucid dream, include experiencing yourself being successful. Suggest that you will recall this feeling when you are actually at work as you find yourself communicating positively and clearly with others.

Study Skills

The first step in improving how you study is to know how your mind creates and remembers images. Take a moment and list what subjects were best for you and how you learned them in relationship to other subjects that were a problem. Take into consideration the learning environments and how you were taught. Now imagine how you would like to study and learn the subjects that are hard for you.

Remember that you can use your lucid dreams to try out any approach to learning you want. Set your intention goals and try them out. Suggest to yourself that you can recall the feeling of being successful when you are actually working on the subject. You can use your learning strengths by changing the images in your mind's eye as you study.

What would it be like to take a test wherever you are the most comfortable? You can when you experience it in your lucid dreams. Imagine stepping outside the pressure of the classroom. You can dream this and recall the experience when you are actually taking a test. All you have to do is imagine what you want to experience in your lucid dreams.

The Power of Suggestion

You have read the term "suggest to yourself" over and over in this book and are now probably used to suggesting to yourself your lucid dream goals during the day and when you are drifting off to sleep or into a lucid dream trance. When you repeat a suggestion over and over to yourself, your unconscious mind absorbs it as a reality. You have been influenced your entire life by suggestions, both positive and negative.

Some suggestions you may have given to yourself, while other suggestions were given to you by both well-meaning and not so well-meaning people. Once a suggestion becomes a reality in your unconscious mind, it stays with you until something or someone creates another suggestion that replaces the old one. Remember, negative suggestions contribute to negative paradigms. Positive suggestions can help create positive paradigms.

When you recall a positive lucid dream experience, you can use the power of suggestion to keep the experience alive in your mind. You can include this suggestion when you are creating your intentions for your lucid dream. You can say to yourself something like, "I will recall my positive lucid dream experience often, and when I am actually doing what I dreamed about. Every time I remember, the experience will feel more real as I achieve my lucid dream goals." Remember to feel gratitude in your heart as you recall your suggestions and lucid dream experiences. Experience these suggestions in all five senses in your mind's eye.

FACT

A posthypnotic suggestion is a suggestion given to a subject in trance with wording that goes something like this: "After you return to your normal waking state, your unconscious mind will remember and give you the same experience as you had during the trance." The goal is to have your unconscious mind constantly reinforcing the trance suggestion.

One of the greatest benefits of lucid dreaming is to be able to use the experiences later as powerful tools to help you achieve your goals. Do you remember the Law of Attraction, the concept that you bring into your life what you sent out? When you continue to recall your lucid dream experiences through the images in your mind's eye, you are essentially re-experiencing your dream. The more you suggest to yourself that what you experienced was real to you, the more the dream will stay with you.

You also need to know and understand that as real as the experiences you have had in your lucid dreams are, they are fantasies, and it is important to make sure your intentions are compatible with the real world that you live in. Lucid dreams only give the experience of realities, some of which may be driven by your ego and not for the greatest good.

Lucid Dream-Suggestion Exercise

This exercise has two parts to it. The first is creating intention suggestions before your lucid dream, and the second contains suggestions to use after the dream. Start by writing down your intentions for your lucid sports-related dream. If it is for athletic ability, decide what you want to improve upon. If it is for another skill, then go through the same process for that.

In your intentions, include the suggestion that you will have a positive experience in your lucid dream that you will recall in full detail with all your senses after the dream is completed. Suggest to yourself that you will recall the feeling of the athletic exercise or event you experienced in your lucid dream in your muscles as well as your mind any time you want in the future. You may also suggest a special word or touch or any other specific action, such as tapping a baseball bat on the ground before you are up to bat, to help you recall the feeling you experienced in your lucid dream.

Part One

Several times a day before your lucid dream, take a breath, exhale, and focus on your lucid dream intentions and suggest to yourself your goals. Keep positive feelings in your heart while your conscious mind stays vigilant as you drift off into sleep. As you are having your lucid dream experience, continue to suggest to yourself that you will fully remember after you wake up.

FACT

Suggested intention: "I look forward to my lucid dream. I will experience my lucid dream to the fullest and remember it vividly after I wake up. Any time I want or need, I can fully recall the positive images of my lucid dream in my mind and with my muscles. I look forward to my lucid athletic dream."

The more you eat, sleep, and "drink," or focus on your goals, the more you are practicing in your mind. You can take a moment any time you want and imagine the feel of a club or a bat in your hand. You can watch your body move as you experience a brief moment in your mind's eye playing a sport or experiencing an activity. You can feel the excitement of what you are doing.

Part Two

The second part of the suggestion exercise is a form of self-hypnosis. Do this several times a day. You can use an anchor such as a keyword, touch, or even a deep breath to start your recall of your lucid dream experience. This exercise will help you go into the zone or an altered state of consciousness trance.

To create an altered state of consciousness trance any time you want, take a deep breath and exhale. Let your mind begin to focus on the images in your lucid dream memory. Feel these images to the fullest and suggest to yourself that whenever you want while you are involved in your sport, you can bring back the positive feelings and emotions of your lucid dream experience. See it, hear it, feel it, taste it, and smell it in your mind's eye, and make it real. Whenever you are ready, you can take a breath and return to full consciousness, fully aware of your surroundings.

As you develop your lucid dreaming skills, you will gain confidence in your ability to use lucid dream experiences to help you achieve your goals. Just as learning the skills of a sport or developing artistic abilities requires a certain amount of dedication, the same is true with your lucid dreaming skills. The willingness to involve yourself daily in the concepts of lucid dreaming can pay off in the long run.

CHAPTER 14

Lose Weight Lucid Dreaming

Here you will you will learn how to create weight-loss goals that you can reinforce when you lucid dream. You will see how it is important to create strong weight-loss images in your mind's eye, and you will look at how you can use dream-induced lucid dreams (DILDs), wake-induced lucid dreams (WILDs), mnemonic-induced lucid dreams (MILDs), and an altered state of consciousness lucid-dream trance to develop a successful weight-control program. You will be shown how to create a mind exercise to help you change your view of food.

Create Weight-Loss Goals

Can you imagine dreaming away excess pounds? Sounds too good to be true, doesn't it? Let's examine how you can use your dream power to change your view of food and help create better eating and exercise habits. There are several ways that you can use your lucid dreams to accomplish your weight-loss goals.

The first step is to identify your weight-loss goals. Ask yourself:

- Why do you want to lose weight?
- How much weight do you want to lose?
- When and where do you overeat?
- How is food important in your life?
- If you lose weight, how will life be different for you and others in your life?

You can use your dream journal to write down the answers to these and perhaps other questions you can think of, but before beginning your lucid dream weight-control program, get your doctor's approval. You may be taking a medicine that contributes to weight gain. Make sure you have a healthy weight-loss plan that provides balance in nutrition and exercise.

Why Do You Want to Lose Weight?

Do you want to lose weight for your own well-being or is it because someone else thinks you are too heavy? Is it for medical reasons or to boost your self-esteem? Sometimes people are pressured by others to lose weight, but when they begin to lose, these same people will try to sabotage the weight loss by tempting them with more food. Sometimes other people are afraid that if you lose the weight you want, you will somehow change and not want them in your life anymore.

How much weight do you want to lose? Are you very overweight or just a few pounds above your goal? Look at lucid dreaming weight control as a lifestyle change. It is the opportunity to change your life for the better. When you create your weight-loss intentions, look at your short- and long-range desires to lose and manage your weight. Remember, you are the master of your food, just as you are the master of your lucid dreams.

What Are Your Eating Habits?

If you are not already, become proactive about the foods you are eating. Know the foods that are going into your body and what is in the food. What are the salt, fat, calorie, and nutrition contents? Are there certain foods that you eat now that are causing your weight gain? Are there foods that you enjoy that promote weight loss?

What are your eating patterns? When do you eat the most? Do you have a tendency to eat a lot of food late in the day? How about exercise? Do you exercise on a regular basis if you are physically able to do so?

Why do you overeat? What purpose does food serve in your life? Some people try to hide in their own bodies and overeat to "protect" themselves. Some people eat for pure enjoyment. Some overeat because of issues earlier in their life or from past lives.

Reaching Your Goal

So if you reach your weight-loss goal, how will life be for you? How will your success affect the lives of others around you? If you lose the weight, what good will it do anyone else besides yourself? If you are motivated for something greater than yourself, it can help boost your heart power. It is sometimes easier to do something for others than yourself.

When a person accomplishes something in his life, such as losing weight, he also begins to see life a little differently. Family members and friends who were associated with him will often feel left out as he goes through his change. Those who don't understand may try to sabotage his improvement so that he will be the way he used to be.

Develop a Strong Weight-Loss Image

Once you have developed your overall weight-loss goals, you are ready to create your intentions to use lucid dreaming to help you reach them. The way you imagine in your five senses in your mind's eye can play a very important part in the way you set your intentions. You have foods that you like that are good for you; you have foods you like that are not good for you; and you have foods that you do not like. If you can change the images in your mind of the foods you like that are bad for you to something you don't like, you can change the way you perceive that food.

Here are some questions to help you define how you can develop a strong weight-loss image that you can incorporate as part of your lucid dream intentions:

- Can you imagine what a spoonful of sugar tastes like by itself? If so, what does it feel like?
- Can you imagine what a spoonful of fat tastes like? If so, what does it feel like?
- Can you imagine the taste, feel, or smell of a spoonful of salt? If so, what is it like?
- Can you think of a food you do not like? Is it the taste, smell, feel, or looks of the food that you don't like?
- Can you see what you currently look like in your mind's eye?
- Can you see what you want to look like in your mind's eye?
- Can you imagine what it would be like if you never lose any weight?

Sugar

Now think of a food that you like that is bad for you. Can you imagine the individual ingredients in the food? For instance, if there is sugar, can you taste the sugar in your mind by itself? It you can, focus on all the sugar in the food in the first taste. The goal is to make the taste or feeling unpleasant and therefore less desirable to you.

Fat

Can you imagine the taste of food that is cooked in fat or has a lot of fat in it? If so, can you imagine the taste, feel, or smell of the fat alone? Now put all of the fat into your first bite. How do you like it now? Of course, the goal here is to make you consciously aware of things you do not like about food you thought you liked. You are more likely to not eat food you don't like.

Salt

You may have found that there are foods that do not have a lot of calories that can still cause you to gain weight because of the amount of salt in it. Can you imagine the taste and feel of a spoonful of salt? Can you imagine all the salt in the food you are about to eat in the first taste? That image alone could be a powerful negative image that makes the food you like undesirable to you.

For a moment, consider all these and other questions and thoughts you have about being in tune with your weight. Imagine in your mind's eye how you would successfully begin and continue a weight-loss and management way of life. Consider all the obstacles that might be in the way and how, through your lucid dreams or lucid dream trances, you could change the obstacles so that you can move forward with your life's purpose.

From a Sleep State

Let's see how you can set your intentions for a positive DILD weight-control experience. To review, a dream-induced lucid dream is one that takes place when you become aware that you are dreaming while you are sleeping. It is a natural occurrence for most people sometime in their lives, even when there has been no intention set to experience a lucid dream. The goal for a DILD dream would be to be open to a lucid dream weight-control experience in relationship to the other things you are doing in your life to promote healthy eating.

The more you are consciously aware of your positive weight-control intentions, the more your intentions are reinforced and absorbed by your unconscious mind. The more your mind focuses on your positive intentions and actions for weight loss and control, the more you are priming your conscious awareness to recognize when you are dreaming so that you can create a lucid dream about losing weight. The benefit of a lucid dream is that you can try out weight-loss ideas and see how they will work as well as look into the future to learn the difference between losing the weight and staying the same or gaining.

Put together your program in your mind, develop your goals, and set your intentions. Here are some hints to help you start priming your DILD "pump":

- **Look at food for what it really is.** Be aware of what's in the food you are eating and where it came from. How much fat, sugar, salt, or other negative ingredients are in it? Make an unhealthy food you enjoy as unpleasant as you can in your mind's eye by being aware of the individual ingredients.

- **Look at healthy food you enjoy.** Experience the positives of these foods versus the negatives of the bad foods. Use your senses to create both powerful positive and negative images of those foods you like and those you dislike.
- **Amplify the negative in the food you like that is contributing to your weight gain.** If there is too much salt, experience the salt. If there is too much fat, try the fat alone in your mind's eye. The goal is to set intentions for eating food you enjoy that is good for you.
- **Let yourself feel good about the food that you eat that you like and that promotes healthy weight loss.** Feel gratitude as you intend several times a day to enjoy healthy food that you like. Intend that as you develop your healthy-eating weight-loss program you will look forward to a DILD experience that will help you understand your past issues with food and how to solve them as you continue to stay in tune with your new approach to positive eating and weight control.

ALERT

Don't wait for a lucid dream to start you on your road to weight loss. Most people dealing with weight have been doing it for much of their lives. Start first and then intend for yourself to be consciously aware when you begin to dream so that you can use the dream for more understanding related to your weight control.

As you develop and progress positively in your weight-control program, take the time to become consciously aware of your intentions several times a day. Repeat these intentions with gratitude as you drift off to sleep at night. If you meditate or do self-hypnosis, experience your powerful weight-control images in your mind's eye through all of your five senses. Be grateful that you also have the opportunity to be consciously aware of your DILDs so that you can use them to further understand how to become in tune with your weight control.

From a Waking State

The more conscious you are of your intentions to lose weight, the easier it will be to use WILDs and MILDs to stay consciously aware of your goals as you drift into sleep. As you recall, a WILD is a lucid dream that you enter from a waking state. Many times a person will wake up while they are having a dream. The dream is very fresh in their mind, but it ended when they woke up. It is possible to re-enter the dream from your waking state.

The more you have consciously worked on your weight-control program during your waking hours, the more aware you will be of your intentions if and when you wake up in the middle of a dream. Chances are if you continually practice your weight-loss images through all five of your senses in your mind's eye, you will have weight control on the surface of your conscious mind. Perhaps you could repeat a slogan to yourself as a weight-loss mantra that might go something like, "Live it. Breathe it. Eat it. Sleep it. Dream it." In other words, keep the concept of weight control in your mind at all times.

Here are some tips for when you wake up in the middle of a dream:

- When you wake up in a dream, take a moment to get your bearings.
- Focus on the dream you were having and experience the memory of it in your mind's eye through your five senses.
- Suggest to yourself, as you imagine that you are back in your dream that you will drift off to sleep staying consciously aware of the dream.
- As you drift off to sleep, stay aware of the dream continuing on, and at that time, do a reality test to prove to yourself that you are dreaming.
- When you have proved to yourself that you are dreaming, take control and begin to dream your weight-control intentions.
- Suggest to yourself that you will fully recall your lucid dream when you wake up afterward.

If you want to have a MILD weight-control experience, define your intentions and repeat them several times a day. When you are ready to enter your sleep period, make yourself comfortable, take a deep comfortable breath, and slowly exhale. Let your eyes go out of focus as you feel gratitude in your heart for the opportunity to work on your weight loss in your lucid dreams. Suggest to yourself that you will continue to be consciously aware as you drift toward sleep. You can remind yourself as you relax your muscles down through your body that you will stay consciously aware as you drift off to sleep and begin to dream.

ALERT

Staying focused on relaxing your muscles as well as your breathing serves to keep your conscious mind alert while you continue to drift toward sleep. It is easy to lose your conscious focus and enter into sleep without your conscious mind staying aware of your intentions, especially if you are tired.

When you have become aware that you are dreaming, do your reality test. Once you know that you are dreaming, you can begin to experience your lucid dream weight-loss intentions. Suggest to yourself that you will fully recall your lucid dream in all five of your senses when you wake up after your dream experience. Write it down in your journal.

From an Altered State

An altered state of consciousness lucid-dream trance can be experienced whenever you have a chance to find a period of time during the day or when you are preparing to go to sleep at night. The length of time could be as short as a few minutes to half an hour. The more you practice an altered state of consciousness trance, the easier and faster it will be to enter it again. Eventually, you may find that all you need to do is get comfortable, take a deep breath and exhale, let your eyes go out of focus, and enter directly into your lucid dream trance state.

FACT

Altered states of consciousness trances are also excellent ways to help reinforce your lucid dream intentions. You can suggest to yourself during a trance that you will be consciously aware when you start to dream. You can record an induction, memorize it and repeat it to yourself as you go into trance, or use a lucid dream trance facilitator.

Create your intentions for your lucid dream trance as usual. Find a comfortable place, take a deep breath, exhale, and let your eyes go out of focus. Suggest to yourself that in a few moments you will count yourself down from five to zero and will enter your lucid dream trance when you reach zero. As you count down, focus on the images in your mind's eye and suggest that when you get to zero, you will begin to experience a lucid dream trance that is related to your intentions for weight loss and control. As you become experienced with this induction technique, suggest to yourself that you may enter your lucid dream trance any time you want as soon as you have taken your first relaxing breath.

Once you enter your lucid dream trance, you are in control and may create positive weight-control experiences to help you achieve your weight-loss goals. You can use imagery to help you change your views of foods that have been problems for you. Suggest to yourself that you will recall your lucid dream trance experiences in vivid detail to help you achieve your weight-loss goals.

Lucid Weight-Loss Exercises

When you establish your intentions to use lucid dreams to help you control your weight, it is the work that you do during your waking hours that will help you set the stage for lucid dream experiences. It is important to change your view of the food you are eating that is not promoting healthy weight loss so that you can make a new mind image model. The more you connect to your new model, the more it becomes part of your unconscious awareness that helps change your eating habits.

Here are some hints that will help you develop an image program during the day that can help prime your mind to be consciously aware of your intentions when you start to dream:

1. **Think of a food you don't like.** Is it because of the look, feel, taste, smell, or possibly the sound of the food? How do you respond to this food when you see it or put it in your mouth? How often do you eat food that you don't care for? Having clear-cut images in your mind's eye of one or more foods that you do not like can be great models for changing your eating habits.

2. **Think of foods and beverages you like that are contributing to your weight gain.** What benefit are these foods giving you? Identify the times that you overeat or eat the wrong foods. How do you feel when you deprive yourself of eating these foods? You may want to write down your answers and thoughts as you formulate your mind-change program.

3. **Think of food and beverages you like that promote healthy weight control.** How do you feel when you eat these foods? How often do you eat them? Are they easy for you to have on hand? Are there any others around you that would not like the healthy foods that are good for you? If so, how could you still eat them without causing disruptions in your life?

4. **Think of the individual ingredients in the food and beverages that are not good for you and identify something that by itself you do not like.** It is important to think of something in foods you have been eating that are bad for you, such as salt, sugar, or fat, that you would not eat as a separate food. Which of your five senses give you the most powerful negative images in your mind's eye? Try each ingredient by itself and experience a strong negative image.

5. **Now amplify what you do not like about a food that's bad for you, imagine it all in the first taste of the food, and compare it to a food that you do not want to put in your mouth.** The goal is to be consciously aware of the negative part of the food even before you put it in your mouth in the same manner as a food you would not normally eat. Try this out in your mind's eye.

Set your intentions to have a lucid dream where you can change the way you have been thinking of the foods that are bad for you. Imagine that you had in front of you all of these "wonderful" foods and beverages that have been sabotaging your weight loss. In your lucid dreams, you can now change these foods into the worst images, based on the way you have already developed your mind's eye negative view of the food through your five senses. Suggest to yourself that you will recall these experiences whenever the negative foods and beverages are temptations for you during your daily and nightly waking hours. Do this exercise several times a day and before you drift off to your lucid dreams.

Keep Track of the Results

For a weight-control program to be successful, there generally needs to be a consistent accounting of where you are currently in relationship to your short- and long-term goals. Diets and weight-loss programs usually work for people as long as they keep daily or weekly track of what they are achieving. You've probably heard the phrase "out of sight, out of mind." Diets usually fail when people have either reached their goals and go back to their old habits or when something distracts them from following their weight-loss plan. Don't beat yourself up when you make wrong choices because that is when you have the opportunity to change the outcome the next time you face a similar situation.

ESSENTIAL

Results often hinge on how well you plan ahead when you decide on the eating and exercise program that is healthy and achievable for you. You want to have healthy food available when you feel the need to eat. When there are no healthy eating options, people often go with poor choices.

For a while, you may want to keep close track of where your weight is and what you are eating. List your successes and failures. Make note as to how you could change a situation the next time it happens, just as a golfer would correct a poor shot in his mind. Remember, just as in a lucid dream, you are in control, not the food. In fact, you can use your lucid dreams to give yourself the feeling of having control over what and how much you eat, and you can recall those feelings to help you as you empower yourself to make the right choices for eating and exercising for weight loss and maintenance.

CHAPTER 15

Lucid Dreaming for Better Health

Lucid dreaming can help you promote better health. Read on to learn how to use lucid dreaming for yourself and others, for animals, and even places. You will also learn how to create negative and positive wellness images. You will experience how to bring the positive images through the negative images to help you dream and recall positive health changes, and you will have the opportunity to try an altered-state lucid dreaming trance exercise.

How Lucid Dreaming Can Help Promote Better Health

As you read through this book, it must seem like lucid dreaming is supposed to be a magic potion that can change, create, and cure almost everything. The fact is that lucid dreaming is not a fix-all formula, but a powerful tool that you can use to help access the goals you are currently trying to reach. The work starts with your goals. Your goals help to identify your intentions.

Your goals should be broken down into two groups: short term and long term. The long-term goals are where you think you want to end up. These goal concepts may or may not change as you make progress toward them. Current conditions in your life may dictate to some extent how you work toward your long-term objectives. In life, you always need to be aware of the realities that work for or against your goals, whereas in lucid dreams you have the opportunity to go beyond reality to experience a long-term goal and look back to see how you got there.

Once you have identified your long-term goal, you can begin to focus on how to get there. Sometimes that seems overwhelming, especially if you are facing a health issue where the main goal is to live. Short-term goals can be as near as your next moment or the end of the day, week, or month. Lucid dreaming can help you begin to link short-term goals together as you work toward reaching your long-term goals.

FACT

"Tunnel vision" is a term that relates to a viewpoint where you can only see straight ahead. In life, tunnel vision is often used to describe someone that is so focused on the future that they are not aware of what is happening to them in the moment.

In health, long- and short-term goals are very important. For someone with a serious health issue, it is hard to establish long-term goals, because she may fear what is ahead in her future. At the same time, it is important to know the reality of the moment. That said, realities can be changed, just as a poor long-term health prognosis may have a different outcome when the power of the mind and positive belief become involved in the goal-setting process. To accomplish what may seem impossible, you need to risk stepping out of your current life realities.

In lucid dreaming, you can step out of your current realities and travel to the future. You can travel to your long-range health goals and see how you got there. As you journey back to where you are now, you can see and experience, if you wish, how your short-term goals affected the outcome. You can try different routes or changes in your short-term goals to provide you the best long-term outcome. There is a lot you can experience in lucid health dreams that can assist you on a positive path to the future.

Dreaming for Yourself

Life situations can often have a strong impact on your health. Your habits, relationships, work, and risk taking can all play a part. Stress plays a large role in your health. When it constantly occupies your mind, it builds and builds. When your mind, body, and spirituality become out of balance, you may become vulnerable to health issues that can have serious consequences. When this happens, you may have lost sight of any goals you may have set.

You can create your intentions to use lucid dreams to help in several aspects of your health. You can lucid dream to understand your current life situation, and you can study it from several different angles. You can experience visually or from other viewpoints. You could go into the future to see what life would be like with and without changes. You can work with your guides and angels to find the right path to good health as well as relationships.

Measured Levels of Stress

The Holmes and Rahe Stress Scale was developed in the 1970s in conjunction with a study of several thousand people dealing with various health issues. The researchers found that stress over a period of time can have an impact on an individual's health.

The study identified forty-three different stress-creating conditions that could impact a person's life and rated the severity of their impact by a numbering system; the more intense the stress, the higher the number. The participants had varying degrees of health issues dating back over the past two years of the study, and identified which of the situations on the list they had experienced. They then added up the numbers assigned to each stress situation. The higher the score, the more likely the participant was to currently have or potentially encounter major health issues. By understanding how they were affected by stress, the participants then had an opportunity to make changes in their lives to help resolve the situation that had created their heath condition.

ESSENTIAL

Once you have identified the cause of stress, you can begin to set your intentions to make changes. Going to a safe place in your mind or in your dreams can help you get a clear picture of where you are in life and help you set your goals for where you would like to go.

When you dream for yourself, chances are that you are thinking of the whole. Remember to feel gratitude and love, even when it seems almost impossible to find. There is always something to be grateful for. Also, remind yourself to feel unconditional love in your heart and to intend to lucid dream for the greater good of the whole. Identify a reason beyond yourself to be in good health, and give yourself permission to dream of miracles.

Create a Mental Image of Your Current Condition

What is your current health condition? It is important to create a mental image of your health through all five of your senses. The goal is to take an abstract concept of how your health presently is and turn it into a three-dimensional image that you can work with to manipulate and change. As you have already learned in this book, you imagine in your mind's eye with two different views. One is experiencing what you are imagining and the other is watching what you are imagining.

Here are some questions to help you assess how you currently perceive your health in your mind's eye:

- **If you have a health issue, can you see a visual image in your mind's eye as to how it looks?** Can you relate it to a color? Perhaps you see your health conditions as a dark or bright red. Can you see an aura connected to it? Can you imagine a negative picture of your current health?

- **Can you imagine what your health situation would sound like in your mind's eye?** You may be able to hear a sound that creates a negative image of what you are currently experiencing. If so, can you turn the volume up or down?

- **Can you feel, at a level that is manageable for you, what your health condition feels like?** Does it feel rough, hard, soft, or spongy? Maybe you can feel a negative sound vibration of what your aura or energy feels like. Can you feel any stress connected with the way your health is at the moment?

- **Can you imagine a smell connected to your health condition?** If you have a good sense of smell, this may be a way to build a mind image of your health. Can you imagine what the smell looks like? Can you recall unhealthy memories related to the smell? Are there any vibrations associated with the smell?

- **Is there a taste that you can connect to your health condition?** For some people taste is a strong sense. Do your negative taste images create any pictures in your mind?

- **Using your five senses, what is the strongest image that you can create that best defines your health issues?** The goal is to create a negative image that becomes three-dimensional in your mind's eye.

ALERT

It can be hard to try to change something when you do not know exactly what you are changing. Once you have created a concept image, you have something concrete to work with.

A three-dimensional image can be one that you see from different angles. If you do not see one, that's okay. Another sense may be able to give you a three-dimensional concept. Even if it is only one dimension or a flat image, that is something you can work with.

Develop a Positive Healthy Image

Now it's time to create an image in your mind's eye of what it is like to be healthy. You may recall some great memories of what your body felt like when you were healthier to assist you in developing strong mind images.

These questions will help you create positive images of wellness:

- **Can you picture a wellness image in your mind's eye?** It may be a memory of what you felt like before any current health condition. If you can, what does it look like? Perhaps you can imagine a healthy color. You may see an aura or even a positive picture.
- **Are there any positive sounds you can associate with wellness?** If you heard a negative sound, you can probably hear a positive one. If you can, can you turn the volume up or down? You may hear a waterfall or the ocean, or nature sounds such as a bird singing. It may be beautiful music playing.
- **Can you feel images related to wellness?** Perhaps you can touch a positive color in your mind's eye and feel its texture. You may feel a positive sound vibration or your aura. You may recall the feeling of a time when your health was better. If so, can you feel what your body felt like then? Can you feel love and gratitude in your heart?
- **Can you imagine a smell that reminds you of wellness?** If so, can you picture what the smell looks like? Are there any vibrations that you can connect with the positive wellness smell?
- **Are there any positive tastes that you can imagine in your mind's eye that relate to wellness?** If so, can you create a picture image of the taste? Does the taste help you recall positive health memories or imagine what they would be like?
- **Combining all of your five senses, what is the most powerful wellness image that you can experience in your mind's eye?** You may be able to imagine in all of your senses or only one or two. No matter how you imagine, that is what is natural for you. Take a moment and experience your positive wellness image.

The purpose of creating a positive mind model of health or a healthy memory is to provide a different view of what one's health is currently like.

The goal is to create a healthy alternative mind's-eye image that can be experienced through lucid dreaming or a lucid dream trance.

A bright and vibrant positive wellness image in your mind's eye and the willingness to focus on it frequently during waking hours will become part of your better health intentions for lucid dreaming. Don't forget to include love and gratitude coupled with heart power. Your ability to imagine with your feeling sense can be a very valuable part of your wellness program. Feelings are like vibrations that can ripple through your body. You'll learn what to do with the ripple in the next section.

Image-Strengthening Exercise

Now let's compare the positive and negative health images together to learn the differences. Look at the visual images in your mind's eye of your current health condition. If for any reason this is too unpleasant, you can always refocus on something else that is healthier. The goal is to help you create an image that you can change in your mind's eye and experience in a lucid dream. The clearer both negative and positive images are, the more you have to work with when you create your wellness intention imagery.

- Focus on the sound of the negative image if there is any, and when you are ready, put that together with your visual picture. Take a moment to get an understanding of how the two are connected.
- Next, use your kinesthetic sense to feel the texture and the mental feeling of your negative health image. Combine this with your negative visual and sound images. Take a moment to understand what you are experiencing.
- Focus on your sense of smell. Can you create a negative smell image of your health situation? If you can, combine it with the visual, sound, and feeling images. Take a moment to evaluate what you are experiencing.
- Do the same thing for your sense of taste.
- Now put all five together to get the clearest image of how your mind's eye imagines your current health situation. Take a moment to evaluate. You do not need to focus on this negative image for long.

It is important for you to have an image concept in your mind of any health issues you may be currently facing.

As unpleasant as poor health images are, when you are able to at least have a concept of what your health issue is in your mind's eye, you have created something that you can begin to mentally manipulate. Once you learn to manipulate the image, you have given yourself options for improving your health.

Now, turn to your positive wellness image.

- How do you visualize your wellness in your mind? Take a moment and see your image or images as clearly as possible.
- Connect to your positive wellness sound image. Combine your visual and sound images together and take a moment to experience them as clearly as possible in your mind's eye.
- Next, feel any textures in your wellness image and experience the positive vibrations you receive from it. You may have more than one image; if you do, just go with the one that is right for you at the moment.
- Now combine your visual, sound, and kinesthetic images together. Take a moment to experience them as vividly as you can in your mind's eye.
- Focus on a positive wellness smell. Take a deep breath and feel it flowing through your body. Combine your smell image with your visual, sound, and kinesthetic images. Take a moment and experience them in your mind.
- Can you imagine a wellness taste? If you can, combine your taste with your other senses and experience them together as vividly as possible in your mind's eye. Take a deep breath as you do this and feel love and gratitude in your heart. Slowly exhale as you continue to feel the positive benefits of your wellness image.
- Now, focus on your negative health image for a moment. In a corner of this image, place a tiny version of your positive wellness image. Take a breath, exhale, and push your tiny wellness image right through the negative one so that all you experience is the positive image. Clear your mind's eye and bring back the negative image and do it again,

feeling the wellness image getting stronger and stronger. Repeat this process five or more times until the negative image does not come back.

Do this exercise once a day or more, if needed. Suggest to yourself that you will continue to feel the wellness image washing the negativity out of your body until the next time you do this exercise. Intend that you will experience this wellness image fully when you have a lucid dream. Intend that your body will respond to the wellness image when you are lucid dreaming and that when you wake up you will recall and your body will respond to the wellness you experienced in your lucid dream.

Preparing for the Lucid Dream

The first step in preparing for your lucid dream for better health is to make sure you have defined your short- and long-term wellness goals. Once you have done this, you are ready to establish your lucid dream intentions. Part of your intentions is your reason for being well. Remember that when you have a purpose beyond yourself, it may be easier to engage your heart power. People often put themselves last because they are focused on helping others.

FACT

You could visit ancient healing temples or crystal palaces and experience mystic healing powers, become one with nature and feel water washing out the negativity in your body, or you could immerse yourself in a healing aura of color and positive energy. With all the possibilities, consider how you will set your intentions for your wellness lucid dream.

Once you enter your lucid dream, you will be able to take control. To prepare for this, consider the different ways you can use lucid dreaming to foster your wellness. You can use the positive wellness image you just created in the last section and really feel it beginning a healing process in your body. You can dream into the future and feel yourself getting better and better as you see yourself getting back to good health. You can suggest to yourself that you will recall this wellness experience in your mind and body when you wake up after your dream.

You can dream backward in your lucid dream to a time when your heath was great and have your body experience it again. You can consult the best doctors and healers in the universe, either living or those that have passed. You can experience their healing and suggest that you recall the positive effects when you wake up from your dreams. You could consult the future for cures that may not yet have been discovered in your lifetime.

Choose Your Lucid Dream Method

Consider how you want to have a lucid dream experience. You can always intend to recognize that you are dreaming in a dream-induced lucid dream experience and be prepared to work on your wellness. You can remind yourself several times a day to be consciously aware of your intentions when you experience a wake-induced lucid dream or a mnemonic-induced lucid dream. You can also work with an altered state of consciousness lucid-dream trance during the day or evening and control your wellness images. Experiencing a wellness lucid dream trance daily can also help promote conscious awareness of when you are dreaming during normal sleep.

You can choose the lucid dreaming technique that you feel will give you the best wellness experience. Remember that it is your willingness to invest your time and patience into creating and experiencing lucid dreams that can help you achieve your wellness goals that may have a positive effect on your overall health.

Lucid Dream Healing for Someone Else

At some time in your life, many of you have probably wished that you had the ability to heal someone connected to you. You may have natural healing talents or have had training in a healing modality such as Reiki. Have you ever thought about dreaming positive thoughts and healing energy for others? Regardless of whether there is proof or not that lucid dreams can bring about healing for others, just being able to do something can help relieve some of your own stress.

Whether you work with healing energy or not, imagine through your five senses how you might offer healing to someone else. In a lucid dream experience, you can feel this energy working to help promote healing. You can see the other person(s) responding and beginning to heal. You can channel the power of the universe, your guides and angels, or your faith to create a powerful lucid dream.

You could scan their bodies as Edgar Cayce did and see what their health problems are, and know how to suggest what they might do to help them with their wellness. You could contact the great healers of the past and present to ask them to help the ones you are intending better health. You could journey into your and their past lives to see what conditions and situations in the past may have contributed to their current health situation. You may imagine other things that you could do in a lucid dream to help promote someone's wellness.

When you work with someone's energy for any reason, including healing, it is a matter of courtesy to get permission from the person before starting. Some people have a belief that does not accept certain types of healings. It may also be good for the person to know that someone cares enough to send healing energy.

You could also use lucid dreaming to help heal animals or even geographical locations. Imagine what it would be like to be able to send loving energy to a part of the world that was filled with strife. In a lucid dream, you have the power to do that. You could dream and see how you and perhaps many others are having a positive affect on a situation or location, close or far away from you. In a lucid dream, you are only limited by the limits you place on yourself.

Lucid Dream Helping-Healing Exercise

Here are two altered state of consciousness lucid-dream wellness exercises that you can use for yourself and for the good of others. These exercises are not meant to take the place of your regular health program and treatments but to compliment them. You can use these exercises to help set your intentions for regular sleep lucid dreams. When you experience a lucid dream trance on a consistent basis, it will help you keep your wellness intentions and goals in your mind as you recall these images experienced during the dream trance.

Exercise 1

Find a good location and make yourself comfortable. Take a deep breath and slowly exhale while you feel positive loving energy flowing over and around your body and through your heart. Let your eyes go out of focus as you experience gratitude for this opportunity to experience a healing lucid dream trance. With each breath, your body relaxes more and more as you prepare to count yourself down to a positive lucid dream wellness trance.

Suggest to yourself as you count down from five to zero that you will drift off into a lucid dream trance where you have complete control of the images you experience in your mind's eye dream state. Continue to breathe in and out slowly as you count yourself down, reinforcing your lucid dream trance intentions and suggesting as you get to zero that you will experience and be in control of positive wellness images in your mind's eye.

Five. Breathe slowly in and out and reinforce your intention, feeling love in your heart as you relax more and more.

Four. Continue to reinforce your suggestions as you slowly breathe in and out and continue counting downward. Three (pause), two (pause), one (pause). As you get to zero, feel yourself entering into your lucid dream trance knowing that you are in control of the images you focus on in your mind's eye.

Zero. You are now in charge of the wellness images that you are experiencing in your mind's eye through all of your five senses. Try pushing a wellness image through an unhealthy one.

When you are ready, count yourself back up from zero to five. Suggest to yourself that you will recall in your mind and experience in your body the healing images you created during your lucid dream trance. You can suggest that every time you experience a lucid wellness dream or a trance dream you will feel the power of your mind working with your body and the other health methods that you are using to help your wellness improve.

Exercise 2

Repeat the first part of Exercise 1, substituting your intentions for others in place of yourself. When you get to zero, focus on your lucid dream intentions toward other people, animals, or locations. When you are ready, count yourself back up from zero to five, suggesting that what you have done will continue to help the intended other(s).

As you develop your lucid dream wellness techniques, they will always be available whenever you want or need to use them. You can dream for a specific purpose or for a general wellness. Perhaps lucid wellness dreaming will become a part of your overall health practice and maintenance plan.

CHAPTER 16

Help Resolve Nightmares Through Lucid Dreaming

In this chapter, you will learn about repetitious and other kinds of nightmares. You will consider what the causes of them might be, from past life experiences to sleeping disorders. You will find out how to use your sources of belief and faith, including your guides or angels, to protect and watch over you as you use lucid dreaming to change your nightmares. You will have the opportunity to try an altered-state lucid dream trance to help resolve past life-related nightmares as well as an exercise to keep nightmares out of your dreams.

Repetitious Nightmares

Most people have experienced nightmares at least occasionally, but you may find yourself facing nightmares with the same theme that repeats over and over, sometimes night after night. For someone who suffers from nightmares, every night is often a night filled with anxiety or terror. They may face each day feeling exhausted from lack of a good night's sleep.

QUESTION

What is a nightmare?
A nightmare is a dream that has a theme of terror, fear, or anxiety. The dreamer usually awakens gripped with the emotions that were experienced in the nightmare. It may take some time to gain composure after waking up from a nightmare.

Perhaps you have a child or know one who has a lot of nightmares. You may have had them yourself when you were young. It is hard to explain to a child that what they are dreaming is not real. Their disrupted sleep can be just as hard on you. You may have felt the anxiety of wanting a child to feel safe and unafraid or you may have had your own night's rest disturbed by a frightened child.

Causes from This Lifetime

What causes a repetitious nightmare? There can be several different reasons. A nightmare may have its roots in a traumatic event that you experienced sometime during your life. If you have experienced such an event, it may replay itself in your mind, both when you are awake and when you dream.

It is possible you may have had an experience sometime in your life that you do not consciously remember that continues to haunt you in your nightmares. Your unconscious mind takes everything in and does remember, playing it out again in your dreams. It is possible that more than one event in your life may trigger your nightmares, so it is feasible that lucid dreaming may help you trace your nightmares back to an earlier incident.

Causes from a Past Lifetime

That earlier incident may not even have been during your current lifetime. You may have suffered a traumatic event in another life that resurfaces in your current life in the form of a nightmare. Past life-influenced nightmares are often experienced by children. They may describe traumatic events that come back in their dreams such as plane crashes, auto accidents, drownings, monsters, and war experiences. Past-life memories are often still close to the surface of a child's conscious mind.

ALERT

> Fears and phobias can be connected to a past-life traumatic situation. When such feelings come on suddenly, they create an altered state of consciousness, similar to a nightmare, except that the person experiencing the trauma is actually hallucinating. You could consider this experience a waking nightmare.

Adults may begin to experience past-life nightmares when something in their current life happens that brings the memory of their past-life experience up to their conscious mind. It may be emotional feelings that are recalled rather than visual images. The emotions from the past may transfer onto an event in the present and make it difficult to identify where the trauma actually began.

Even if you never really identify the roots of your repeating nightmares, you can resolve them in a lucid dream. You can go back into your past lives and heal the trauma. A past-life facilitator can do this when he induces a lucid dream-like trance during an altered state of consciousness. You can also accomplish it yourself or use any other lucid dream technique to help end a repetitious nightmare.

Different Nightmares with the Same Theme

It is also possible to experience nightmares that are different every time but still have a connection through a similar theme. For instance, you might always be running away from something. In one dream it might be an animal such as a tiger, lion, or a bear that is trying to get you. In another it might be a bad guy that is doing the chasing. The result is that you usually wake up with your heart pounding.

These dreams may be caused by stress in your life or even by certain types of medication. Sometimes, your system is trying to make adjustments to medicine that you may have started taking or stopped taking. Other health conditions can cause nightmares. Your body may be sending you a message through your nightmares to pay attention to yourself.

Digestion and Dreams

Certain food eaten too late in the day can contribute to dreams and nightmares. For instance, wine or carbohydrates can turn to sugar and cause your heart rate to increase while you are sleeping. If this occurs during REM, chances are that you will experience a nightmare and you will wake up with your heart pounding. As you become older, your metabolism can change and foods that never affected you may now cause nightmares. It is important to know how your system works and to avoid foods that may cause you a problem during the night.

Even your sleeping position can affect how you dream. If you suffer from acid reflux, you may well be aware of this already. You may find that acid reflux is contributing to your nightmares. Always check with your health care provider regarding any medical question you may have—in this case, regarding digestion.

Psychic Dreams

It may be that you are psychic, and the images you receive in your mind's eye could cause you to have a nightmare. Some people dream of tragic events that come true in the future. They may dream of plane crashes or wars. They may dream that a member of their family, a friend, or even a famous person is going to die. It could be a natural death or some kind of tragic event. Dreams are a time when the psychic's mind is often open to information she would not always pick up when she is awake.

Psychic dreams are often intense and, because of their nature, can cause anxiety for the dreamer. When a child or teenager has tragic psychic dreams, they often feel somehow responsible for events that actually happen. Consequently, they try to suppress their psychic abilities and often live and sleep in fear that they will have another dream about tragedy.

ESSENTIAL

You may have had too many dreams in your life that have contained psychic information to dismiss the fact that something is coming to you. If this is the case for you and you are uncomfortable with it, ask your guides to only give you dreams that have information that give you positive insights.

Facing Your Fears

As you can see, there may be different causes for your nightmares. You can be affected by your past, whether in this life or in lives before. You can be affected by the present. It could be your present living conditions, working situation, or relationships that cause you anxiety. You can be affected by fear of the future and all that is unknown.

Random nightmares can happen at any time. Think how great it would be to be able to change any of your bad dreams into positive ones. You actually can through lucid dreaming. You can develop a technique to help you be ready when you become aware that you are having a nightmare or even when you wake up from one. This technique will help you be ready to face and change your negative dreams.

Setting Intentions for the Lucid Dream

Here are two specific sets of intentions to help you prepare for a lucid dream that changes a nightmare or any type of negative dream. The first set of intentions is to help you resolve a repetitive nightmare. This can be done through the usual lucid dreaming techniques or through an altered state of consciousness lucid-dream trance.

If you have or are suffering from nightmares, have you kept an account of them in your dream journal? Here are some questions you can ask yourself that may help you get an idea of your nightmare pattern.

- **How often do you experience nightmares?** Every night, once a week, once a month, certain times of the year, or just randomly? Even if you have not kept a record of when they occur, you may be able to recall some approximate times over the last year or more.
- **Is there a pattern of events or other situations or conditions that precede a nightmare?** What was going on in your life before your nightmare? Was there additional stress? What did you eat, drink, read, watch on TV? Who did you talk to? Were they friends, relatives, adversaries? How is your general health? What medicine are you taking, drugs or homeopathic remedies? Was anything special happening at work or home?
- **Can you identify when your nightmares first started?** How long ago? How old were you? What happened in your life just before the first one?
- **Do you have any medical issues that might contribute to a nightmare?** Do you have sleep apnea? If you are struggling to get air when you are sleeping, it may cause you to experience a nightmare.
- **Could your sleep position contribute to your nightmares?** Simply changing your sleep position may help eliminate nightmares.

Understanding how you experience your nightmares can help you set clearer goals of definitive intentions. Some of your nightmares may not be resolved through lucid dreaming. Nightmares that are caused by food, medicine, or other stimulants that speed up your pulse rate are created by an actual physical condition.

Intentions for Random Nightmares

The second set of intentions is for dream-induced lucid dreams, wake-induced lucid dreams, and mnemonic-induced lucid dreams. They are designed to help you not only be consciously aware of when you are experiencing a nightmare or negative dream but how to change those types of dreams into positive ones. You can prepare for these experiences as you would prepare for the possibility of a situation that may or may not happen in your life. You might think of it as defensive driving in your sleep.

These intentions can be used to help work with random nightmares or ones that may have a common theme. You can answer the same questions regarding repetitive nightmares to help you understand what you have been experiencing. However, the intentions you are now creating are for nightmares that could happen at any time.

Knowing You're Awake and Not Alone in the Lucid Dream

Another very positive factor that you can bring into play when you experience a nightmare is your faith or belief in a power—in something or someone that watches over you. It is not easy facing the world alone, especially in the dark of a nightmare. Just knowing in your mind that you are not alone as you face and change your nightmares and negative dreams can be of great comfort. There are a couple of ways that you can incorporate your belief in making positive changes through a lucid dream.

Once you are confident that there really is something with you, you can establish an intention that your conscious mind will always know that you are not alone. As you repeat this to yourself, feel love and gratitude that you are being watched over, not only while you sleep but at all other times. Regardless of what is going on in your life, faith can be a positive force that helps you carry the weight of life so you don't have to feel the need to hold up the whole world.

Protective Intentions

A prayer can be an intention. Wording your prayers with gratitude and love can help strengthen your intention. Remember the Law of Attraction: you get back what you send out. Knowing when you wake up in the middle of the night that you are surrounded with something positive and protective may help you find peace of mind.

You can use your protection intention many times a day. It could be when you are traveling, working, or in the shower. You can use your intention as a mantra. The more you consciously repeat it, the more powerful it will become in your unconscious mind. When you need it, it will automatically come into your conscious mind.

You can also set an intention that you will be consciously aware of not being alone when you encounter a negative dream or a nightmare. You can intend that you will test the reality of the dream, surround yourself with the elements that go with you, change the nightmare, and create a positive outcome. You can intend that when you wake up after having experienced a nightmare, you will put yourself back into it, surrounded by the protective team that goes with you. Once you prove to yourself that you are dreaming, you can go about changing the negative dream or nightmare.

ESSENTIAL

A gratitude protection intention: "Thank you (fill in the blank: God, angels, guides, etc.) for watching over me and guiding me as I go through this day. Thank you for being with me and watching over me as I sleep. Thank you for helping me face and change any nightmares that I may encounter in my dreams."

Changing the Nightmare Through Lucid Dreaming

There are many ways you can change a nightmare through your lucid dreaming because you know that it isn't real and that you are not alone. Here are some ideas to consider, ways that you could make changes during a lucid dream. It really boils down to what approach works for you that is comfortable and feels right. By thinking about what you might use and imagining what the positive results would be, you are bringing your intentions into your conscious awareness.

You can become invisible, watch your nightmare, and contact help to get rid of the bad parts. You can create a protective shield that blocks the nightmare from returning and tests the outcome in your dream. You can journey back in time to the beginning of the nightmare and change the beginning by creating a different dream. You can shrink giants down to nothing or blast the bad guys with powerful laser beams.

If you wake up in a war, you can go back in time and create peace. If you are starving, you can create an abundance of food. If you are cold, you can move the dream to a peaceful warm place. If you wake up in another time period, you can come back to the present. If you are dying, you can go back before the scene to change the outcome and the negative situation.

ALERT

If you are psychically dreaming of something negative in the future, you can ask your team to help change the results by taking the right actions during your waking life to help change the negative outcomes of your psychic dreams. You may also intend that you only dream psychically of things that you can have a positive effect on.

Childhood Nightmares

Perhaps you have or know of a child plagued by nightmares who could benefit by knowing that they can change them so that they won't come back. If you do, you can have them identify what is safe and protective to them. It may be a parent, friend, stuffed toy, or something known only to their mind's eye. It doesn't make any difference what they choose, as long as they have a strong feeling of protection associated with it. Focus on their positive images before looking at the negative.

Have them imagine their superhero being with them at all times, watching over and protecting them, especially when they dream. Have them imagine waking up from a nightmare and knowing that they have a superhero that is going into the dream to change it. Have them imagine watching this happen. Suggest to them that they are now always safe and protected and free from their nightmare.

A Guided Altered-State Nightmare Resolution

A guided altered state of consciousness lucid-dream trance can also prove to be a valuable technique in helping someone eliminate nightmares that have plagued him for a long time. This method is especially good for a repetitious nightmare that may be connected to one or more past lives. You could create your own guided imagery or go to a professional such as a hypnotist that can guide you through your lucid dream-like trance process.

You will experience your trance differently than anyone else because of the way you process images in your mind's eye. You may be able to watch the process like a dream movie, experience the dream trance while it is taking place, or be able to do both.

If your nightmare is connected to another time period, the goal is to go back and understand what happened. Then, either change the outcome or go back before the negativity started. When you have found something positive in the past, you can connect to that character or part of your soul and bring positive healing and resolution to the outcome.

Here is a past-life nightmare-resolution lucid-dream trance exercise that you may try. You can use it like it is, change it, or create an entirely different one.

- Take a few moments and get comfortable in the place where you would like to try this exercise. Take a deep breath and slowly exhale. Continue to do this as you feel gratitude and love in your heart for the protective team that surrounds and helps you to resolve and heal issues from your past that surface in your nightmares.

- Let yourself feel safe and protected as your eyes go out of focus and your muscles begin to relax, starting at the top of your head and working your way downward to your feet. Remind yourself of your intentions to experience a lucid dream trance that lets you change, heal, and resolve your nightmares in a positive way.

- When you are ready, begin to count yourself downward from five to zero, suggesting to yourself as you do that you will remain consciously aware as you drift into your lucid dream trance. You will be watched over and protected by your team the whole time you are in your lucid dream trance as well as before and afterward.

- Suggest to yourself that when you reach zero, you will recall an image in your mind's eye of a past nightmare, and you will be able to watch the image as a movie in your mind. You will also be able to step in and out of the images to learn the reason for the nightmares.

- As you slowly count down, remind yourself of your intentions, repeating your suggestions in between each count. Five (pause). Four (pause). Three (pause). Two (pause). One (pause). Zero (pause). When you get to zero, feel yourself surrounded by your protective team. Focus on the images that come into your mind's eye.

- Now go to a place in the images before the nightmare starts. It could be a happy time in the life of the character that you experienced in the nightmare. See this character. Look through their eyes as if you were the person you saw in your mind's eye. What do their clothes look and feel like? How does their hair look and feel? What do they have on their feet? What is the temperature and time of day? What is their mood? Are there any sounds, smells, or tastes? What is happening around them?
- Watch the images as if in a movie as they go forward to when the cause of your nightmare began. Did the character in your mind's eye die there or was it another time? Move forward to when they died and know their last thoughts without experiencing it physically.
- You now have the option of changing the scene or going back to a happier time period and connecting that experience to you as you are now. Bring healing over the negative outcome with your heart power of love and gratitude. For a moment, move forward in your life to see how what you've learned can help you in the future.

Now go back in time and check to see if there were other episodes that are contributing to your nightmares. If there are more, do the same exercise until they have all been resolved. Dream your way forward again and experience sleep without any nightmares. Suggest to yourself as you count slowly back from zero to five that you will continue to remember that you have resolved and healed your old nightmare. Feel gratitude and love as you come back to the surface of your conscious mind, fully aware of where you are and of feeling relaxed and positive.

Helping Make Sure the Change Is Permanent

Finally, after your lucid dream trance is over, suggest to yourself that you will continue to be surrounded by the love and support of your team wherever you go or whenever you dream in your sleep. Every day, remind yourself that you are grateful to be free of the old nightmares. Many times a day stop and take a breath and feel the positive energy that surrounds you.

Define what the nightmare used to be like in your mind's eye. Create a positive protective image through all five of your senses. Take a few moments and feel this image with gratitude and love. Now bring back the negative image.

FACT

Practice makes perfect. The more you practice positive mind's-eye imagery that includes unconditional love and gratitude, the more it will become a part of your total self. Once the unconscious mind has absorbed the message of unconditional love and gratitude, you will recall and experience the message in your conscious mind, just as you intended to do.

Place a small positive image in the big negative one. Now push the positive one through the negative to push it away. Bring back the negative and repeat the process until there is no room for the negative image to return. Take a breath, exhale, and feel gratitude that you are now free from your old negative images and dreams. Doing this exercise once a day may help keep the nightmare "boogie man" away.

CHAPTER 17

Travel in Your Lucid Dreams

Now you will learn how to create a lucid dream travel plan to preview a trip that you would like to take or flying without a plane. You can experience the culture of your destination through your five senses, and you will consider the importance of a lucid dream travel journal. You will also have the opportunity to try an exercise to visit a family member or friend through a lucid dream trance.

Create a Travel Plan

There are lots of fun things you can do in your lucid dreams, including travel. You may do this naturally nearly every night or you may have found yourself traveling in your dreams when you didn't want to. Flying dreams are one of the most common lucid dreams. Unfortunately, many people who become aware that they are flying in a dream don't realize that they can control what is taking place. When an experience like this happens, the dreamer is more often than not just along for the ride.

With the knowledge about lucid dreaming that you have acquired so far in this book, it may not take long to become a frequent flyer in your dreams. You can prepare yourself in case you have random flying lucid dreams or you can set intentions to have specific lucid dream travel experiences. You will look at both concepts.

ALERT

A flying dream is a traveling dream. You may or may not go far, but you may experience a floating sensation and possibly see visual images that place you somewhere in the air, sky, or outer space. This experience usually takes place with the awareness that your body or your astral body is floating by itself.

You may have had other types of dreams where you became aware that you were flying in a plane or something else. Some of these dreams may be connected to past life situations that surfaced while you were sleeping. Can you think back over your life and identify how many or how often you have experienced traveling or flying dreams? Were there any reoccurring or theme-related dreams about traveling or flying? You might want to add these memories to your dream journal.

Past Experience

You may have experienced nightmares where traveling was usually the theme. If it was a repetitive dream, especially from a different time period, it may be a past-life experience that ended traumatically. If that is the case, you can use your favored techniques to resolve the nightmare. As you uncover more about past-life traveling dreams, you are also beginning to establish, through conscious awareness, goals for future ones.

Just as any traveler uses past experiences to help him prepare for his next journey, your previous travel dream experiences can help you create travel plans for your next lucid travel dream. By reviewing past experiences, you may become aware of pitfalls to avoid in the future. If you have experienced lucid travel dreams before, you may not have known that you could control them. Now you do.

Reasons for Lucid Traveling

Take a moment and identify in your mind how you would like to integrate lucid dream traveling into your life. Start with what you already know through past experiences. Then intend to practice floating or lifting off in a lucid dream while you keep firmly tethered to the ground with a silver cord that will only let you float a little until you are ready for longer flights.

Here are some questions to help you create a travel plan:

- **Do you want to fly in your lucid dreams?** Perhaps you want to learn to control your flying and have an out-of-body or celestial-body experience. You may have had lucid dreams in the past where you weren't in control and would like to learn how to be. If that is the case, you can set your lucid dream intentions to take flying lessons.
- **Do you want to go back in your life to a different period in the past or travel to a past life?** You may want to travel with your mind to revisit events that have taken place in this life. You may want to visit a time period that you have questions about or wished you had lived in. You may want to examine a past life.
- **Do you want to visit people or places in your lucid travel dreams?** You may want to check up on a family member or drop into a favorite location. You may be traveling and want to check up on your own home or pet.
- **Do you want to travel to a place that you have never visited before?** Perhaps you want to see what it is like in a location you would like to visit in the future.
- **Do you just want to travel for fun?** Maybe you just want to go on a lucid dream vacation. You don't even have to pick a destination until

you start to lucid dream. You are free to create any travel adventure you choose.

You may have other lucid dream travel ideas. Make notes in your journal. Choose your destination and create your lucid dream travel intentions.

Go Where You've Always Wanted to Go

So where would you like to go? You have a ticket that is good for any lucid dream destination you want to choose. What is your first choice? Take a moment, if you haven't already, and just imagine where you want to go.

You may want to visit a place you have never visited before and currently know little about before you do any research on the location. This could prove to be a good test of the accuracy of your lucid dream traveling. You can compare the experience you had in your lucid dream with any research that you do afterward. Remember that some people have a natural psychic ability to travel in their minds, as Edgar Cayce did, while others may find it harder to visit unknown places in their lucid dreams and be able to accurately describe them. If the actual locations and experiences in your dreams don't exactly match, don't worry; you may dream differently than other people do.

FACT

You may find that you have a natural psychic ability similar to Edgar Cayce's and are able to travel in a lucid dream or lucid dream trance to unknown locations. If so, congratulations for this incredible gift. You can develop it until it gives you many insights that you might use to help others who are not as fortunate.

Once you have decided, there are a couple of ways that you can go about approaching your journey. Your destination may be one that you have been to before and you want to go back and enjoy some more. If you are already familiar with where you are going, there will be few surprises or discoveries unless you decide to visit it differently than when you were there before.

Check Out a Vacation Spot

Maybe you have chosen a place to visit that you have never been to before. If this is the case, you may or may not know much about the experiences you will have when you experience your lucid dream. You may want to do some research before you set your intentions to visit in your lucid dreams. If you choose to investigate before you create your intentions for your lucid dream, you may want to learn about the terrain, climate, people, and culture. Familiarizing yourself with your destination before you go is like making any other travel plans.

You can use your lucid dream to see if what you have planned to take on your trip is the right stuff. You can find out if the clothes you have chosen will be comfortable and appropriate for your journey. You can check out anything that might be worrying you about an actual trip by taking it ahead of time. Lucid dreaming can help you begin to feel more comfortable about the destinations you want to travel to by letting you check out the unknowns that you may encounter as you actually travel there in your future.

Help for Making a Decision

Maybe you would rather travel to a college to check it out and sit in on some classes. You can experience what campus life is like and how the professors teach their courses. You can sample dorm life and meet other students to find out how you want to live during your college years. You might want to dream what it's like to go on a cruise and take a tour before you actually book one. You can use lucid dreaming as a predestination travel tool.

FACT

Patty always regretted that she was unable to attend college after she finished high school. She maintained her passion for learning all during her working life, and after she retired, she started to go to college in her dreams. She chose an ivy-covered brick building, and she monitored the classes inside during her lucid dreams.

As you can see, there are countless ways that you can check out destinations in your lucid dream. It can be a specific location or an unknown location. You could actually visit a place in a lucid dream and try to figure out where you are. You can play a game like "stump the dreamer," where you go someplace unknown and guess where you are. If it sounds like fun, give it a try.

Sample the Culture Through All of Your Senses

Part of your "stump the dreamer game" may be to sample the culture of the dream location. You can try anything or any custom you want in your lucid dream. Here are some reminders to help you set your intentions to recall the memories in your mind's eye of a complete cultural experience in the location you have chosen.

Visual Image Lucid Dream Experiences

Create your intentions to include both experiences and observations through all five of your senses during and after the dream. Once you become aware that you are dreaming and have proven to yourself that it is a dream, you are ready to become part of the cultural experience of your dream.

When you arrive at your destination, observe it from a distance to get an overall perspective of what is going on. Remind yourself that you will be able to fully recall everything you observe and experience in this lucid dream location. You can move about any way you want, either seen or unseen.

ESSENTIAL

Remember that in your mind's eye you will recall experiences through your five senses: seeing, hearing, feeling, tasting, smelling. Even if you dream visually, you may not recall the memory visually. You may just have a "knowing" what it would be like to have a visual experience.

Now, if it is appropriate, step into the culture and make note of what things look like. You may observe people, buildings, or scenery. Check out the modes of transportation. Look for any other visual information that can help you understand what the culture is like in your lucid dream and remind yourself that you will recall the information fully in your mind's eye when you awaken.

Auditory Lucid Dream Experiences

What do you hear in your lucid cultural travel dream? Make note of the language being spoken. In your dream, you can even understand foreign words. Can you find a place where music is being performed? Can you hear birds, animals, or water? What other sounds can you experience and then recall after you awaken?

Kinesthetic Lucid Dream Cultural Experiences

What are your feelings about the places you are visiting? Is there happiness or sadness? Experience the temperature and the time of season. Note the time of day or night that you are visiting. Is there anything that you can touch?

Olfactory Lucid Dream Cultural Experiences

Can you distinguish any smells in your lucid cultural dream? Perhaps you can experience the smell of foods being prepared or served. You may make note of location smells or move around in your dream, experiencing all the different smells. Suggest to yourself while you are there that you will be able to fully recall and describe any smells you experience in your cultural travels.

Gustatory Lucid Dream Cultural Experiences

Are there any foods in the culture you are visiting that you can taste? You may want to walk through a market, sampling as you go, or sit down at a restaurant and eat a full meal. You can dine with the locals to experience what it is like to be there through all of your senses. You can travel to different locations and try the local fare and bring back a recipe in your memory to prepare in the future.

Include in your suggestions that you will fully recall your lucid dream cultural experience through all five of your senses when you wake up. Make some notes in your dream journal after you wake up and take more time as soon as possible to write up your experience as fully as you can remember it.

You can prepare some questions covering your five senses to help jog your lucid dream-experience recall. Be prepared to make note of any further details you remember about your lucid dream over the next few days.

Visit Family Members

Have you ever thought about visiting family members through lucid dreaming? Perhaps you are related to someone that is living far away, either permanently or for a specific period of time. They may be in a branch of the armed services or away at college. Then again, maybe you are the one that is away from home, and you yearn to just drop in for a visit.

You may have someone that you are connected to who is ill, and you wish you could help him heal or give him comfort. You may want to check on the welfare of someone close to you or be present at a family gathering. You may have someone that is in a concert, a play, or a sporting event that you are not able to physically attend. Perhaps you have someone missing in your family, and lucid dreaming may provide some clues to their disappearance. There is no limit to how you can use your lucid dreams to connect to your family.

FACT

Here is an experiment that you can try during your lucid dream trance. Ask the person that you are going to visit to leave something at a prearranged spot for you to observe while you are there. It could be an object, a serving of food, or even a piece of paper with a couple of words on it.

You might plan for a family member to meet you in your dreams. Although you can do this with dream-induced lucid dreams (DILDs), wake-induced lucid dreams (WILDs), and mnemonic-induced lucid dreams (MILDs), you can also choose a time for each of you to induce your own altered state of consciousness lucid-dream trance for meeting in your mind's eye. This method can incorporate your psychic abilities and those of your family member to create a strong connection during your dream trances. It can also prove much faster than the traditional lucid dreaming methods and at the same time help you become consciously aware of the possibility that when you are dreaming, you can contact or visit a family member.

A Plan to Meet

You can try this altered state of consciousness lucid-dream exercise with a family member or a friend. It is important that both of you are aware of your goals and have set the same intentions for this dream trance experience. To start, you may want to visit them or ask them to visit you. As you progress, you can try meeting on an astral plane. It can be a fun project, and you may learn that you have an ability to travel in your lucid dream trances.

- Once you have chosen a time to connect, make yourself comfortable and prepare to enter into a lucid dream trance state. Take a deep breath and slowly exhale, feeling gratitude and love in your heart. Suggest to yourself that you will connect with the person you intend to meet when you enter into your lucid dream trance. Let your eyes go out of focus and continue to breathe slowly in and out. You can begin to relax your muscle groups from the top of your head down to the bottom of your feet, as you remain consciously aware of your lucid dream trance intentions.
- Count yourself slowly down from five to zero, suggesting that you will become consciously aware of your lucid dream trance when you reach zero. As you count down, let yourself drift deeper and deeper into your lucid dream trance with each count. Five (pause). Four (pause). Three (pause). Two (pause). One (pause). Zero (pause).
- When you reach zero, being consciously aware, look at your hand, look away, and let yourself see a different background as you look at your hand again. Suggest to yourself that you are aware and that you are now ready to take control of your lucid dream trance.
- When you are ready, let the images in your mind's eye focus on the person that you want to visit. You may see or feel yourself traveling there or just picture the scene in your mind, using the imagery of your senses.

- Now let yourself be aware that you are connected to the other person. Let images come into your mind to see, hear, feel, smell, and taste what might be there. If you can see the person, take note of what they are wearing or doing.
- After you have finished your visit, suggest to yourself that you will recall all the details. Count yourself back up to five, completely aware of your surroundings.

Here are a couple of other suggestions that you can try with one or more other people during a lucid dream trance experience. You might prearrange to meet out in the astral plane at a specified time or place—have a party or play a round of golf. Try to actually communicate with them and compare notes afterward. Remember, in a lucid dream trance, anything is possible.

Keep a Travel Journal

You may want to have a travel journal separate from your dream journal to keep a record of your experiences. In some ways, it's no different than putting a scrapbook together of a trip that you have taken. If you have artistic ability, you could even include your mind's-eye snapshots of adventures you experienced on your lucid dream journeys. You can write descriptions of your memories through your senses, recalling sights, sounds, emotions, smells, and tastes you encountered in your dream travels.

You can even create a relaxation exercise to help you recall your lucid dream travel experiences. These memories may be created through traditional lucid dreaming techniques or through an altered state of consciousness lucid-dream trance. Make note of when and how you experienced your lucid dream when you write up the adventure in your travel journal. You may find that your journeys will make a great subject for a larger writing project in the future.

Recall Exercise

Find a comfortable place where you will be relaxed and at the same time ready to type or write. Center yourself with a deep breath, exhale slowly, and feel gratitude in your heart for the lucid dream memories that will come into focus in your mind's eye. Let the images of your lucid dream experience come into your mind and experience them in all five of your senses.

You may want to pause every so often to let your memory screen reload with more information. You can rerun a scene or part of a scene any time you want to get more recall information. When you reload, more details often come through than were there the first time.

Now, write down what you are experiencing. Remember to include visual descriptions, sounds, touch, and emotional feelings, smells, and tastes. You can feel like you are there again as you describe what is coming into your mind's eye.

Don't worry about the amount of information you are getting. It may be just a little bit when you begin, but as you get used to priming your unconscious mind to open up to your memories, it will begin to flow easier. The more you practice remembering, the more you will open up to the lucid dreaming information inside your mind.

Traveling Lucid Dream Exercise

You can also travel in a lucid dream the same way you can in real life. You can take a train, a boat, a plane, or any other mode of transportation to reach your destination. You can travel using any lucid dream technique you choose, depending on what works the best for you. You may be a natural at DILDs and often consciously find yourself somewhere near the end of your sleep period, experiencing a dream that continues on while you interact with it. Some people do this all the time without realizing that they are lucid dreaming.

FACT

Janet loved to travel and kept detailed journals of her experiences. In the wintertime on a cold dark evening, she would often sit back in her chair and induce a lucid dream trance state that let her relive a past trip. She looked forward to the journeys in her mind.

You may find a WILD or MILD works best for you. You can adapt any of the exercises, especially the lucid dream trance exercises for preparing for regular dreams. You can count yourself off to sleep suggesting that you intend to become consciously aware when you begin to dream. Once you have proven that it is a dream, you are free to travel if you wish. If you wake up in a dream, you can imagine that you are still dreaming and stay consciously aware as you go back to sleep while the dream is still going on. Always suggest to yourself that you will fully recall your lucid dream when you wake up after it is over.

Here is an exercise for a lucid travel dream that you could use to prepare for an actual trip or a dream just for fun:

- Create your intentions to take a trip. Make your plans and repeat them several times during your waking hours and again as you prepare to sleep or experience a lucid dream trance.
- Get comfortable, take a deep breath, and feel unconditional love and gratitude in your heart as you repeat your lucid dream intentions.
- Let your eyes go out of focus as you begin to relax the muscles in your body, starting with the top of your head and continuing downward.
- As you continue to breathe easily and relax, repeat your intentions to experience a trip in your lucid dream as you drift into sleep.
- Remind yourself that you will be consciously aware when you start to dream and will be able to prove to yourself that you are dreaming. Continue to relax until you fall asleep.
- When you become aware that you are dreaming, do a reality test, and when you are ready, start your travel adventure by planning and packing.
- Next, begin your journey on your choice of transportation. You can cover a day's journey in an instant in a lucid dream and still remember the whole day.
- Follow your itinerary and return home when you're ready, suggesting to yourself that you will fully recall your travel experiences after you wake up.

You can also use this technique with any traditional lucid dream method. As you can see, there are a lot of different ways that you can have lucid dream travel experiences. Your only travel restrictions are the limitations you set for yourself.

CHAPTER 18

Explore the World of Mysticism and Spirituality

Because you have progressed in your lucid dreaming skills, now you'll learn how to induce a shamanic lucid dream. You will find a lucid dream exercise to help you connect to the core of the universe and journey back along a silver cord to the beginning of your soul and experience oneness. You will examine how your lucid dream experiences may strengthen your faith. You will learn how to receive advice from your guides on the astral plane and have mystical experiences.

Shamanic Journeying

Shamanic journeying has been practiced for at least 20,000 years by cultures throughout the world. The origin of shamanism is believed to have started in Siberia and Central Asia, although similar customs were in existence at the same time by peoples that had no contact with Asia or Siberia. Early shamans in different cultures served as healers, medicine men, witch doctors, mystics, sorcerers, and diviners, to name a few.

A shaman has the ability to exist in two worlds: one is in the ordinary reality of the normal world and the other is in the reality of the cosmos (universe), where the astral body is free to journey, work with healing spirits, and take on the forms of plants and animals. If you are interested in studying shamanic journeying, see the website references in the back of this book to help you investigate the subject further.

Aids for Shamanic Journeying

Essentially, a shamanic journeyer uses an altered state of consciousness trance through which he enters into the reality of the cosmos. He is often aided into trance by the rhythmic beating of drums. It could be one or more drums, or it might be other rhythm instruments, such as shakers. Chanting can also be used by itself or with the drums. The repetitious sounds and rhythms help induce the participant into his trance state.

Native Americans use drums with dancing and chanting to bring about altered states of consciousness. Sweat lodges also work in a similar way, through heat and sweat, which cause the participants to begin to experience hallucinations. Vision quests may employ fasting. All of these rituals have their roots in earlier shamanic practices.

Preparing for a Shamanic Journey

The best way to prepare for a lucid dream shamanic journey is to first research shamanism so that you have an idea of how it has been historically practiced, and then set your intentions for a lucid shamanic dream. You could take on the form of an animal and experience what it feels like. You can learn the wisdom of plants or journey into the underworld or visit guardian spirits that watch over you.

You can take a shamanic lucid dream journey to virtually anywhere you choose for any reason you want, whether it is spiritual enlightenment or healing for yourself or others. The difference between normal lucid dream traveling and shamanic lucid dreaming is that you shift from ordinary reality to nonordinary reality. In the nonordinary or shamanic state, you are free to experience the cosmos for many different perspectives, all relating back to your dream goals and intentions.

QUESTION

What is the underworld?
In shamanism, the underworld is a place below the earth's surface where power animals are believed to exist and can be connected with. It is where humans come from and return to after death, and is a destination in a shamanic journey known as the lower world.

An altered state lucid dream trance is an excellent way to begin your shamanic journeying. You can use recorded drums or other sounds to help you enter your lucid dream trance. You can also vocalize sounds such as "ohm," sing, or repeat a chant or mantra. As you do this, induce a lucid dream trance in yourself. As you drift off into your lucid dream trance, remind yourself that you will fully recall your shamanic journey after you awaken and come back to the surface of your conscious mind, fully aware of your normal state of reality.

Back to the Beginning

Suppose you could go back to the beginning. Just where do you think the beginning is? Perhaps you have an idea in your mind, but maybe you aren't really sure what you believe. Belief is a major component in the way that you set your intentions to go back to the beginning. Then again, if there is a beginning, how do you set a goal to return there?

When you think about it, each moment is a beginning and an ending. The human body regenerates almost all of its cells every seven years. We are constantly changing not only our body but our mind and spiritual thoughts as well. Many people use the change of seasons or the first of a new year or their birthdays to begin anew. As much as we would wish to, it is impossible to start again with a blank slate because we still remember our past in our minds.

How Do You Go Back?

Some people believe that each person has a soul that lives many lifetimes. Therefore, the beginning would go back to the creation of a soul. If that is the case, how does one retrace her journey from where she is currently along her soul's map back to her origins? You may want to go back even further than the beginning of your soul. You may want to go back to the beginning of the universe.

FACT

Some people consider each life as a life by itself. It starts with birth and ends with death. There is a beginning, and there will be an ending etched in their belief system until something happens that causes them to question what they thought was true. This belief is held by many western religions.

That seems like a long way to travel. Does that mean that you have to go through every lifetime backward to get to where you came from and to where the universe began? You can if you want to, but there are other ways to go back to the beginning. There are several different regression techniques to help you go back to your beginnings.

The word *regression* means "to go back to an earlier point of time." Some people actually act as they did when they were younger without being aware that they are doing so. In hypnosis, you can regress to an earlier place in your present life, to a past life, as far as your soul's beginning, or even further.

Follow the Silver Cord

One regression technique is to journey along the silver cord or thread that spiritually connects your soul to its beginning. The cord itself is anchored to the location that the soul is currently at, which is you. There is no chance that this cord will get disconnected, and you are free to travel along it as far as you want, knowing that you can safely return to where you are now. You can stop along this cord or thread anywhere you choose to investigate and learn from your past lives. You are traveling in spirit or with your astral body, so your physical body is safely grounded to the earth.

Visit the Akashic Records

Another regression technique is to journey out to the Akashic records, where the history of your soul is housed in the library or the Hall of Records. You may travel, like Edgar Cayce, through a tunnel and on to the library. When you are at the book with the history of your soul, you can open it yourself or be guided to the information by the guardians of the library. You can choose a past life to examine or go back to the beginning of your soul and from there back to the beginnings of the universe.

Download the Knowledge

If you are nonvisual, you may choose to go back to the beginning of your knowing. You can download the knowledge of the history of how your soul started its journey. Even if you do not see in your mind's eye, you may be able to give a detailed description through what you know in your mind's eye. You may act as a channel for a universal source and relay what comes into your mind in the moment without any previous thought about what comes through you.

Guided Tour

You can also let yourself be shown your beginning by your guides or angels or whatever you believe is there with you as your soul travels through space and time. They may take you on a tour and let you experience what it was like at the inception of your soul. They may tell you the story so that it will be in your conscious mind when you come back to a normal waking state.

You can choose any of these methods, choose another one, or create one yourself to help you travel back to your beginning or the beginning of the universe. You don't have to go all the way back at first. You can start by getting the feel of it as you try out different lucid dream techniques and develop your goals. You may want to go to a past life and even between lives to examine your soul's purpose in different lifetimes. You may want to experience a shamanic dream and travel out into the cosmos.

Connecting to the Core of the Universe

Have you established your goals for a lucid dream that can take you back to the beginning? If not, take a few moments and do that now. It is a good idea to use your dream journal to keep a record of your goals. Once you have set your goals for your dream experience, include them as part of your lucid dream intentions. Make sure that your intentions are worded simply and clearly. Once you have finished setting your goals and creating your intentions, you are ready to experience your lucid dream.

ESSENTIAL

This is a reminder of why consciously repeating your lucid dream intentions is important. The more you consciously repeat a thought, the more you are reinforcing them in your unconscious mind. The goal is to have your unconscious mind return the memory automatically to your conscious mind when you are dreaming, so that you will be aware of your intentions.

Remind yourself of your intentions several times a day before you plan to experience your lucid dream. Also, do your reality check and remind yourself that you will be consciously aware when you begin to dream so that you can prove to yourself that you are dreaming and that you have the ability to take control and experience what you have intended to. The goal of this exercise is to take you back to the beginning of your soul. You can experience it as a lucid dream trance or use it to help you create a dream-induced lucid dream (DILD), wake-induced lucid dream (WILD), or mnemonic-induced lucid dream (MILD). When you are ready, choose the place and time for your lucid dream experience.

Start the Connection

Take a moment and focus on your breathing. As you breathe in, let yourself feel gratitude and unconditional love in your heart. As you slowly exhale, remind yourself of your lucid dream intentions and feel them flowing through your heart out into the universe. Let your eyes go out of focus as you continue breathing in and out. You may allow your muscles to relax from the top of your head downward to the bottoms of your feet.

Continue to feel your lucid dream intentions flow through your heart with gratitude and love. Remind yourself that as you drift off into sleep or a lucid-dream trance, your conscious mind will be fully aware of when you begin to dream. You may slowly count yourself from five down to zero, surrounded by love and support from your team that watches over you. You may also remind yourself that you will experience your lucid dream through all five of your senses and will be able to fully recall your experiences after you wake up from your dream.

You may begin to sleep or enter your dream trance even before you finish counting down. The more you practice this exercise, the easier it will be to enter into a lucid dream or dream trance. Five (pause). Four (pause). Three (pause). Two (pause). One (pause). Zero (pause). Your conscious mind is fully aware that you are now drifting into sleep. In a short while, you will be aware of your dream and will know that you are dreaming and be ready to take control.

Journey Back

Now that you are ready, using the regression technique that works best for you, prepare yourself to journey back to the beginning of your soul. Use the silver thread or cord method for this exercise. Use the senses that work best for you. If you visualize in your mind's eye, you may see the silver cord and observe yourself as your astral body starts to float upward with a firm connection to the cord. Watch what is taking place, and at the same time, feel and know that you are journeying back to the beginning of your soul. As you journey upward, be aware of your lifetimes that you are passing over and the core of energy and light you are approaching.

You may observe yourself not only as a human but also in other life forms as you continue to travel backward along your silver cord. You may be aware as you get closer to the beginning that you have shed any physical forms that you experienced earlier on your journey back to your creation. You may feel peace and incredible love as you draw closer and closer. You may be aware of a powerful peaceful energy and experience it in colors, sounds, vibrations, emotions, smells, or even tastes.

FACT

The silver cord is thought to be the connection between your soul and your physical body. The cord is connected at birth and severed at death. While it is connected to the body, the soul can travel along the cord into spiritual realms.

Experiencing the Meaning of Oneness

You are now at the beginning of your soul. Go back to just before you were created. You are able to experience your creation through your lucid dream experience or lucid dream trance from two different dimensions. First, feel the oneness of universal energy and love. At this point, you are one with the whole. Experience what this feels like and ask that this information will be able to be translated into words, pictures, sounds, feelings, smells, and tastes that can bring an awareness to others that might benefit from your lucid dream experience.

Suggest to yourself as you are having this incredible experience that you will fully recall in all five of your senses and be able to clearly describe, in human terms, your journey into oneness. Now, when you are ready, feel yourself becoming an individual soul in energy form, fully balanced as male and female and with all the knowledge of the oneness. Take a moment and watch this incredible event happen as if you were in a movie theater in your mind's eye. As you are watching, you are also free to step in and out of the scene so that you can experience anything that you feel the need to experience.

Observations

Let yourself observe how the oneness of everything in the universe relates to how you are now in this stage of your soul's journey. Continue to watch and experience as your soul begins its migration through the universe. Now move forward along your silver cord to the time when your soul begins to incarnate into physical forms. Take note at that first point of incarnation and look for the possibility that your souls may have divided into two physical forms, a male and a female. Could you observe something like this happening as you took on a physical form?

What were your early incarnation experiences like? Did you experience other places besides earth? If you found that you divided into two souls, how do your various lifetimes intertwine? What happens between lifetimes? Where does the soul go?

ESSENTIAL

It is not necessary to review or know everything in one lucid dream experience. Remember to constantly remind yourself that you will recall in vivid details your lucid dream oneness experiences after you wake up from your lucid dream. You may find that you have an ongoing research project as you continue to work with your lucid dreams.

You can both watch yourself and feel yourself in all your senses as you now begin your journey back down the silver cord and back into your body, filled with the peaceful loving energy of oneness. As you travel back, you may make note of past lifetimes that you would like to visit in one of your future lucid dream experiences.

Come Back

When you are ready, if you are experiencing an altered state lucid dream trance, you may come back to the surface of your mind, fully aware of your surroundings. If you are using this exercise as a means of inducing a lucid dream, you may experience your dream as suggested. You will have full recall of your lucid dream oneness and the beginning of your soul experience and be able to accurately translate it through your five mind's-eye image senses. Take your time to record all the details in your dream journal.

Strengthening Your Faith

How did your lucid dream oneness experience relate to your faith or belief? Did your dream provide confirmation or create a conflict with what you may have been taught to believe as you grew up? If so, what was confirmed for you? What may have caused you to question what you experienced in your lucid dream? Make sure that you give all of your feelings or emotions a voice in your dream journal.

FACT

Faith is the trust and belief in something that you cannot actually prove exists. It is often connected to religion and spirituality. For example, the Law of Attraction is based on the faith that your thoughts are real and will produce the desired results.

It is very possible that you experienced what you intended to experience in your lucid dream and that for the most part it was compatible with what you currently believe in. You are and were, after all, in control of your lucid dream. You may have changed the images you encountered along your journey to oneness without knowing it. That doesn't make any difference if you work with your guides to receive the right ones for you when it is the right time.

More Questions than Answers?

What does matter is what you may have been able to take away from the experience that can help strengthen your faith. If you are a Christian, your experiences may have reinforced your faith. If you have another religious belief, then look for what in the experience may have strengthened what you already know. If you are spiritual, how did your experience relate to what you believe? If you have no faith, what was the experience like for you?

On the other hand, if you have been questioning what you were taught to believe, what was your experience like? Did your lucid dream create more questions upon awakening or did you find something that you can investigate in future lucid dreams or trances? There is nothing wrong with running into more questions as you look to define what is acceptable to you relating to your faith. The goal was to take you back to a connection in your soul with the oneness of the universe.

Peace and Love

Your experience may encourage you to find ways to connect to this oneness on a daily basis. You do have the ability to recall your lucid dream experience. If you found something positive, take some time at least once a day and reconnect to it. Just take a deep breath, feel gratitude and love in your heart, and as you exhale, journey out on your silver cord to the oneness of the universe. Feel its peace and love.

You can do this as a daily intention and be ready to be consciously aware when you have your next lucid dream. You can pause for a brief moment, leave, and come back, and nobody will even be aware that you left. If you are in your car, you will always stay focused on your driving. Your daily intentions can become part of your gratitude and oneness loving energy that you feel in your heart and help you to be connected with all. It is a place in your mind's eye to take and deposit your worries and consult with the beings that watch over and guide you.

Seek Advice from Your Guides

You can also meet with your team on the astral or spiritual plane through lucid dreaming. The first step is to set down your goals for meeting with your guides. Why do you want to connect with them? Perhaps you would just like to have a conversation out of curiosity or maybe you have a pressing problem that you need help and advice for. It makes no difference because you can create your intentions any way you desire. Remember to write them down clearly and to the point in your dream journal.

Were you able to actually communicate in any past dreams or was the subject of your dream doing all the conversing? Did you meet them on an astral plane or did they visit you as you slept? Were you familiar with lucid dreaming when you had this experience, and if you were, did you do a reality check? What did you learn from your past experience that can help you prepare for your next lucid dream?

ALERT

Perhaps you already connect with something on the astral plane that may come to you in your dreams. You may have experienced visits from your guides, angels, or loved ones who have passed over. The experience may have been so real that it is hard to know whether it was a dream or an actual visitation.

Once you have set your intentions, remind yourself several times a day as you prepare for either a lucid dream or an altered state of consciousness lucid-dream trance that connects you to your guides. Your intentions may include the questions you want to ask when you become aware that you are ready to meet them in your lucid dream. You can adapt the induction technique to fit with your intention. You can also prepare yourself to have a DILD, WILD, or MILD experience, reminding yourself that you will fully recall your lucid dream when you wake up afterward.

Guided Lucid Dream Mystic Journeys

Finally, you can use your lucid dreams to visit the nonordinary realities of the mystics. You can connect with the realms of the universe that go back to its very beginning, even further back than the beginning of your soul. You can visit the far reaches of the cosmos to gather the meaning of life and creation itself. There is no limit to what you can connect to and experience through your lucid dreams.

You can start by dreaming an overview of the meaning of life or you can establish a specific goal that you would like to investigate. You may have already researched mystics and mysticism and have a definite idea of what you would like to experience. If you have not, you can always do a little research before you create your lucid dream intentions. You can also step into the shoes of a mystic in your dream. You can know their thoughts and learn how they learned to connect with the wisdoms of the universe.

FACT

> If you are interested in mysticism, you may want to find a copy of *The Urantia Book*. It is a complex history of the universe that was originally channeled by an unknown source(s) between 1934 and 1935. It was not published until 1955, and is a book of over 2,000 pages.

Once you have set your intentions, repeat them to yourself during your waking hours, remind yourself to be consciously aware when you begin to dream, and that you will fully recall your mystical lucid dreams after you wake up or return to full consciousness from a lucid dream trance. Once you have had a mystical experience, you can always recall it and reconnect any time you want for more guidance and wisdom. All you have to do is take a breath, feel gratitude and love in your heart, and open your mind's eye to the mystical guidance that is there for you whenever you want or need it.

Enhance Your Psychic Abilities

You may not know this, but you may be a psychic medium and may be able to talk with loved ones on the Other Side through your lucid dreams. Here, you will consider how you can psychically consult with your guides and dream the future before it happens. You will also consider remote viewing, how to heal the past (whether in this lifetime or previous ones through healing love), visit the Akashic Records, and consult with the great minds of the cosmos.

Talk to Loved Ones on the Other Side

You have probably noticed that many aspects of lucid dreaming are integrated into more than one part of your life. Now you will consider how your psychic abilities can be tapped into and used in your lucid dreams. First on the agenda is to determine how your natural psychic abilities are already influencing you, whether you know it or not. You are psychic, as everyone is in his own way. No one receives psychic information in exactly the same way.

Your psychic information comes to you through your mind's eye in the same way that you recall your memories. You may experience psychic information related to yourself or others. It may be about the past, the present, or the future. Many people have past-life dreams or premonition dreams about the future. You may have experienced one or both of these types. You may have dreamed of loved ones that have passed to the Other Side.

FACT

Psychic information is information that would not normally be available to you to know. It comes to you through nonordinary channels. You may see an image in your mind's eye that gives you information, hear a voice or other sounds, get a feeling somewhere in your body, or experience a smell or a taste.

Chances are that you have been receiving psychic guidance in your mind's eye for a good part of your life, even though you may not have noticed it. You may want to take some time and write down all the unexplainable experiences you have had in your life that might be of a psychic nature. Include any dreams you may have had and knowings such as when the phone was going to ring or who was calling. You may have looked at someone and saw colors around them. If you have, that means that you can see someone's energy called an aura.

Are You a Medium?

Perhaps you are a medium and don't even know it. A medium is a psychic who also has the ability to connect to the Other Side. All mediums are psychic, but not all psychics are mediums. Have you ever looked at someone and seen images of figures around or in back of them? If you have never tried it, have someone stand or sit in a position for a couple of minutes, as you gaze just off to the side of their head and not directly at them.

Were you able to see anything? If you did, take a moment and mentally ask them to show you a sign of how they are related or connected to the person you were looking at. When you relay that information, the person may identify the images with someone on the Other Side. You may hear in your mind's eye the information from the deceased or from your guide. You may get a smell or a taste that the subject of your observation may recognize as connected to someone they know that has died. You may even receive direct messages from the Other Side for yourself or to pass on to someone else.

Meeting in Your Dreams

If you have dreamed about someone who has passed, were you just dreaming or were you receiving a communication from the Other Side? The right answer to that question is how you feel about it. What do you believe? What is a real experience to you might not be to someone else. Learn to trust in the truth, knowing that you may not be able to explain it to others.

If you want to meet a loved one from the Other Side in a lucid dream, set your intentions, remind yourself several times a day, and choose the lucid dream technique that works best for you. Remind yourself that you will be consciously aware when you start to dream and feel gratitude that you will have the opportunity to connect with a loved one. When you are aware that you are dreaming, perform your reality check and know that you are free to connect. You can ask them questions, receive advice, and perhaps get messages to give others that are missed by the subject of your lucid dream. Suggest to yourself that you will fully recall your lucid dream experience when you wake up after the dream.

Consult with Your Guides

You may already be in the habit of consulting your guides on a regular basis. If not, you may want to consider giving it a try. Some people will receive daily guidance during their last period of REM in the night just before they wake up for the day. Their guides may give them creative ideas, suggestions for the day, or other types of useful information that they can depend on. Your guide may be a religious figure that you recognize or a spiritual being that brings you comfort and joy. They are always available to connect to you in your lucid dreams.

ESSENTIAL

You may or may not know who your guide is. If you don't, that's okay. All you need to do is believe that you have something watching over you. It may help you to remember the times in your life when something may have been looking out for you.

You may have had dreams in the past that contained psychic information where you either just knew or heard a voice telling you. You may have had a being or an angel appear to you when you slept, giving you information about the future or about someone else. They may be delivering a message from someone that has passed or from a spiritual source. You may receive a warning of a future tragic event that helps you take an alternative action to change the outcome.

Making Contact

To consult your guides, write down your intentions in your dream journal and repeat them to yourself several times a day. It is best to have a specific reason so that you can focus on it during your waking hours. Remember to feel unconditional love in your heart and gratitude that your guides are there to consult with you. Continue this feeling as you anticipate the positive guidance that you will receive in your lucid dream. Choose the lucid dream or altered state lucid dream trance method that works best for you.

Remind yourself of your intention as you prepare for sleep by taking a deep breath and slowly exhaling. Intend that you will be consciously aware when you begin to dream. If you wake up in the middle of a dream, let your mind's eye review what you dreamed and imagine that you are back in the dream. Stay consciously aware as you drift back to sleep to continue the dream. When you realize that you are dreaming, perform your reality check to prove to yourself that you are in a dream.

Take Control

You are now ready to take control of your dream and call in your spirit guides. They may come to visit you or you may go to visit them. Ask them what you intended to ask. You may actually talk with them or communicate on an astral plane where you will receive a knowing. It is possible that they may not have an exact answer for you during this dream. It may come later in another dream, while you are awake, or it may happen in other ways such as a situation being taken care of for you without your needing to get involved.

Knowing that you always have someone or something to consult with can be a great comfort. It doesn't have to be a major problem or situation. If you want, you can just check in and consult with your guides on a regular basis to help you live your life.

Visit the Future

Perhaps you are a time traveler and have a natural ability in your mind's eye to journey through the veil of Now into the past or future. You may have done so in your dreams whether you wanted to or not. It may have happened to you during a certain time in your life when you received more than one dream about the future.

ALERT

When a young person experiences future dreams with unsettling images, she often lives in fear that she may have more of them or that they are somehow connected to dreamed events that came true. One of the values of being able to lucid dream is to know that, regardless of what you are dreaming, you have the ability to change the dream.

If you become aware that you are experiencing a negative future dream, you are not stuck with the images in the dream. If you are dreaming, do a reality check when you become consciously aware to prove that it is a dream. Once you have proved that you are dreaming, you are in control. You can go forward to and observe the potential outcome of the dream, and then you can come back and create a new chain of events that leads to a different and positive ending. It really doesn't matter whether you have changed the future or if you were in a fantasy, as long as the future happens without the negative outcome that you first dreamed about.

You may want to visit the future through a lucid dream for a specific reason or for curiosity. If you have a natural ability, you may want to use a lucid dream trance. In many ways, that's what a psychic does. She goes into an altered state of consciousness and experiences the future. The images she receives may be specifically for the person she is reading or may be a general predication of events that appear to her in her mind's eye.

A psychic gets her images just as you do, through her five senses. She may see the future, get the information from a higher source such as her guides, or just know the future. She may receive smells that relate to someone connected to the reading. She also may receive taste images. Just like you, she may process her mind's images in all the senses or in just one or two.

What Will Tomorrow Bring?

Set your intentions for a futuristic lucid dream. You may want to know what tomorrow holds in store or want to visit future lifetimes. You can visit with your astral body or just be an observer and look into a window of the future. Once you have set your intentions, choose the lucid dream technique that you would like to use and consciously prepare for your future lucid dream experience. Remember to use your heart power of unconditional love and gratitude that you will have the right future lucid dream for you at this time, and continue to be consciously aware when you start to dream.

Follow the lucid dream techniques you have learned in this book as you prepare for your experience. If you want, you can use your silver cord to visit the future. When you have proved that you are in a dream, you are ready to journey up the cord and out into the future. You can stop anywhere, whether it is only one day ahead or in another lifetime. When you are ready, you may return, knowing that you will fully recall your future lucid dream when you wake up afterward or come back to full consciousness after your lucid dream trance.

Heal the Past

You know that lucid dreaming can help improve your physical health. You can also use your psychic ability to go back and heal the past. It may be that you want to heal the negative memory of a personal experience, a family situation, or a geographic location. If it is something that has been bothering you, set your dream intentions. When a dream occurs and you have proved to yourself that you are dreaming, go back to the situation and watch it unfold so that you can get a clear view of what took place. Regardless of whose fault it may or may not have been, connect to your healing intentions and bring unconditional love into your dream, letting it flow over all the negative images of the past.

Suggest to yourself that this loving energy will help heal the events of the past and regardless of anyone else's views, you are now at peace and ready to move on into the future. Suggest to yourself while you are there that you will continue to recall this peaceful, loving, healing image in your mind's eye with gratitude in your heart as you move forward. Send this same love, regardless of how you may feel about them, to anyone else who was in your lucid dream. Suggest that whenever the thought of this situation or experience comes up in the future, all you need to do is take a breath and connect to the healing love that is in your heart.

ESSENTIAL

You can use unconditional loving-heart energy during a lucid dream to heal an event that took place in the past. It could be the site of a battle, a natural disaster, or some other traumatic situation. If you are visual, you may want to send a healing color over the darker memory. Use all five of your senses.

Intend to go back to that time in a lucid dream, and after you have identified the negative energy that is still there, let the unconditional love in your heart flow over the other with gratitude, and watch the healing take place. Remind yourself that you will continue to feel the healing any time you think of that place and situation.

How the Past Can Heal the Present

It is even possible to use a past-life lucid dream to help create healing images for that life and your current life as well. Your lucid dream intention may simply be to go back to a past life that may be negatively impacting this one. You may or may not know what or when that life was. Once you have taken control of your dream, you can journey out on your silver cord to a past life that is connected to a condition in your current life.

Once you have located that life, observe the conditions that are impacting you now. Go to the end of that lifetime and see how you died, and then know your last thoughts just before you passed. Once you have accomplished that, go back to a happy time in that life before the conditions that impact you now began. In your lucid dream, take the hand of that person in their happy time, bring them to where you are now, and feel your selves bond together with love and gratitude in your heart. Let that love flow over the past life conditions that are impacting you now, and feel this loving healing energy heal the scars from the past as well as the present.

Remote Viewing

You can use your psychic ability to eavesdrop on a specific location. You may have a natural psychic ability to astral project or somehow project your mind's eye to coordinates of exact locations around the world and be able to give an accurate account of what is actually there. Even if you are new to remote viewing, you can experience it during a lucid dream.

FACT

The United States Army developed and experimented with a remote viewing program from the late 1970s through the mid 1990s, when the funding for the program was dropped. One of the program's goals was to be able to observe locations around the world that were of particular homeland security interest to the military.

Today, psychics use remote viewing to help solve a crime or look for lost people and items. Some are excellent profilers and have the ability to look through the eyes of a criminal and develop a personality profile of how they think, what their habits are, and why they commit their crimes. The object here is not to encourage you to spy on someone, but to use your gifts to help people and animals. If you visit someone remotely, make sure you have her permission before you "drop in."

You may be able to find a lost pet or object by using your lucid dreams and psychic ability to project yourself to the area where it disappeared. To try remote viewing, create your lucid dream intentions, remind yourself of them during your waking hours, feel gratitude that you will go to the right place, choose the technique you want to use, and prepare to recognize when you begin to dream. You can get an overview and then begin to narrow your search until you find where your objective is currently located. If you are a natural, you may be able to do a lot of good for others through your psychic lucid dreaming.

Send Healing and Love

You can also use your psychic ability in your lucid dreams to send healing energy and love to friends and family. You may already be familiar with and trained in a healing modality such as Reiki. If you are not, you may want to investigate by experiencing a session, attending a demonstration, or researching the subject. The more you develop your natural psychic healing abilities in your waking life, the more it will help you send healing and love in your lucid dreams and altered state of consciousness lucid-dream trances.

You may have been a healer in a past life. If you want to find out, create an intention to travel out on your silver cord during a lucid dream to a life in the past where you were a healer. You can ask your guides to take you to the right lifetime and show you the key moments of that life. Go to a time when the healer was at his best and experience what it feels like to you so that you can re-establish the healing memory in your consciousness. Then go forward in the healer's life to the point where he died to see if there were any traumas that may have carried over to you.

Know what the last thoughts were in that life and consider how they relate to your current life. Now go back to the best and happiest time in that life and merge it with gratitude and love. Bring healing ability through that life all the way along the silver cord to where you are now. Suggest to yourself that when you wake up after your dream or come to full consciousness after your lucid dream trance, you will clearly be able to recall your healing gifts from the past and be able to integrate them into your life now.

Meet Great Minds in the Cosmos

Finally, how would you like to get together with the great minds of the cosmos? You can also do that through your lucid dreams. Imagine for a moment that there is a wise council out there somewhere in the universe that knows the answer to every question posed by man or any other intelligent being. What if this was a place where ideas could be freely exchanged without the fear of ridicule? You just may be able to journey there in your lucid dreams.

Perhaps you can think of someone in history that you've always admired and wished you could have known. If you can think of one or more, create an intention to meet them. Several times a day, imagine what it is going to be like, even to the point of actually meeting them. Experience your intentions with gratitude and unconditional loving-heart power. Every time you do this, you are priming your mind for the lucid dream experience.

FACT

Don't worry if you have already researched the history of the character that you are interested in; that shouldn't prejudice the experience. Chances are that you already have a connection to this personality and may have known them before, anyway.

Go through your usual lucid dream or dream trance preparation and choose a meeting time. Once you have proved you are dreaming, you are free to travel out into the cosmos and confer with the great minds you intended to meet. Suggest to yourself that you will fully recall your lucid dream experience with the great mind(s) you consulted when you wake up or come back to full consciousness after the lucid dream has ended. The wisdom of the cosmos is always there waiting for you to access it.

CHAPTER 20

The Fantasy World of Lucid Dreaming

In this chapter, you will learn about the benefits of experiencing lucid dream fantasies. You will have a chance to examine the wide range of dream topics that you can choose from and the pitfalls of having lucid dream fantasies flow over into everyday waking life. You will discover how you can step into the shoes of anyone you might want to be, and try a lucid dream fantasy exercise.

The Benefits of Lucid Dream Fantasies

Many people who know how to lucid dream or those who have learned how use lucid dreaming for pure enjoyment. It is an opportunity for them to act out their fantasies in their dreams or revisit great memories from their pasts. There are no rules or consequences in lucid dreaming. You are free to create any type of scenario you desire. That said, it is also imperative to know that you are experiencing a dream that is not real. Life and reality outside of the lucid dream fantasy may be very different from what you experienced within it.

QUESTION

What is a fantasy?
A fantasy is defined as free-flowing thoughts that have no constraints. They can be positive or negative and can develop into so-called hallucinations when the imaginer has trouble separating fantasy from reality. Fantasies can also be a productive way to solve problems "outside the box."

Perhaps you have already been creating fantasy lucid dreams. If so, where have you gone, what have you done, and how has it affected your waking life? It is also possible that you have already naturally experienced lucid dream fantasies at some point in your life.

Sexual Fantasies

Teenagers and young adults often experience sexual fantasy lucid dreams. They appear naturally at a time when sexual energy has built up inside the dreamer. This type of lucid dream is usually unplanned, and the dreamer suddenly becomes consciously aware that the dream is still happening. His conscious awareness may kick in just before the energy of the dream reaches its peak, which is usually just before the time he wakes up.

Lucid dream fantasies can actually be a way for the dreamer to release thoughts and emotions that have built up in the mind. Whether it is releasing sexual energy or getting rid of frustrations, lucid dreaming can provide a lot of positive benefits for the dreamer that can carry over into his waking life. Lucid dream fantasies may help bring a balance to your life in a therapeutic way.

Adventurous Fantasies

For some people, a lucid dream is a way for them to have adventures they would never be able to have during their normal waking life. They can take a rocket ship to the moon or dive to the depths of an ocean. They can go back in time to experience what it was like to live history. They can journey into the future and experience what it will be like.

If you are a writer, you can use a lucid dream fantasy to experience a story and then recall it later as the basis for a book. You can play out a scene from several different perspectives. You can look through the eyes of one or all of the characters in the story, knowing how they think and how each one experiences. When you have finished your lucid dream, you can suggest to yourself that you can always take a few moments, create a lucid dream trance, and step back into the story. Learning to instantly recall your last scene will help you let the story continue as you are writing it.

Successful Fantasies

Basically, anything that you can imagine in your mind can become a reality in a lucid dream where you are consciously aware that what you are experiencing is not real. Knowing that your lucid dream is not real and setting clear intentions beforehand to stay consciously aware and to recall fully in your mind's eye after you have woken up from your fantasy may provide you with a different perspective to produce positive outcomes. Successful fantasies need to be created on a solid base of reality to keep the balance.

So as you can see, there are many benefits to creating fantasies in your lucid dreams. Whether it's for pure pleasure, to help solve a problem, or for creative ideas, lucid dreaming is definitely an option that can enrich your life. You can set your intentions for a fantasy dream. You can be prepared to take control when you become aware of a normal dream fantasy occurring. You can also experience an altered state of consciousness lucid dream fantasy anytime you want by scheduling some time to experience it.

What Type of Fantasy Do You Want?

So what type of fantasy would you like to experience in a lucid dream? The only limitations are the barriers you create in your own mind. Your mind has a tremendous amount of creative ability, especially when connected to your belief system. This is especially true of your fantasy dreams that are intended to help you improve something related to yourself.

Milton Erickson, a psychiatrist and clinical hypnotherapist, and one of the inspirations for the development of neurolinguistic programming (NLP), nearly died from polio at age seventeen. While he lay in his bed on his father's farm, almost totally paralyzed, he began to use his mind to fantasize that he was able to get out of bed and move. He practiced this altered state of consciousness trance day after day, his body began to respond to the images in his mind's eye, and he eventually walked again.

FACT

Milton Erickson became a well-respected psychiatrist who was able to induce his patients into waking trances in which their minds were shown a different view of their situation. His techniques could be interpreted as a way of inducing an altered state of consciousness lucid dream for helping his patients move forward in their lives.

Are You Looking for Fun and Relaxation?

If this is your goal, consider the type of fun you want. It could be a romantic fantasy. You could be the star in your own movie and be a hero or the world's greatest lover. You can create any kind of adventure you desire. You can come back time and time again to the same lucid dream if you want and rewind it.

Are You Trying to Solve a Problem?

You can study a problem from any angle you want in a lucid dream. You can fantasize different solutions created by the different strategies you experienced in your dream. You can use your psychic abilities to look into the future to see how this situation will play out over time. You have complete freedom to try anything you want to solve a current problem, or you can ask your guides to show you the best way for it to be resolved.

Do You Want to Improve a Skill?

You can create a fantasy sport or artistic training camp in your lucid dreams and fantasize your improvement. As you continue to dream your intentions, you may find that you are in fact accomplishing what you have been fantasizing about, especially if you suggest to yourself that your muscles will fully recall how you felt in your lucid dream experience.

Do You Want to Improve Your Health?

Fantasies should be whimsical and fun, and it might be good for you to take a less serious approach to improving your health. You can do things you used to do that you may not be able to at the moment through a lucid dream fantasy that couples enjoyment with health improvement by creating pleasant scenarios in your lucid dreams.

ESSENTIAL

Remember that even in a fantasy lucid dream, if you have a purpose for the greater good that you can believe in with gratitude in your heart, it will help stimulate your conscious awareness to recognize when you are experiencing a normal dream. Once you prove to yourself that you are dreaming, you are ready to fantasize.

What else would you like to accomplish in a lucid dream fantasy? Perhaps you have something completely different in mind, maybe something that you have always wanted to be. If you know what that is, you can set your dream goals to experience it. You can do or be anything you want to be in your lucid dream fantasy.

False Realities Can Carry Over into a Waking State

Some people have natural fantasy-prone personalities. They have the gift of being able to create such powerful images in their mind's eye that sometimes it is difficult for them to draw the line between fantasy and reality. These types of individuals are usually good hypnotic subjects because they accept suggestions given to them by a hypnotist to change their perception of reality. In other words, they will believe and act like a chicken when it is suggested that they are a chicken.

If the person who thought he was a chicken had been given the suggestion that he would remain a chicken after he was brought out of his trance, he would continue to act like a chicken. Why? Because he was still in a trance, even though he thought that he was consciously aware. Applying this concept to life, there are people who go about in a form of trance where they seem normal, but they may be seeing reality completely different from the world's interpretation of reality. Because they are in their trance, they may not realize that they are out of touch with reality.

Manifest and Unmanifest Reality

Edgar Cayce spoke of two kinds of reality: manifest reality and unmanifest reality. Manifest reality is everything that is physically provable to exist such as actual chickens. Unmanifest reality is also real but exists on a plane that others can't prove to exist.

Unmanifest reality applies to people who have psychic abilities of seeing, hearing, feeling, tasting, and smelling energies that are real but on a different frequency and therefore not easily accepted by others. Thus, there is a constant conflict between what is fantasy and what may be unmanifest reality that is real to the person who experiences it.

Perhaps you can understand how difficult it can be to be psychic and live in a society that does not accept what psychics know as real. At the same time, if a person thinks she is experiencing a reality that isn't real, it can lead to a lot of problems. It is just as important to maintain a conscious awareness while you are awake as it is when you become aware that you are dreaming. In other words, it is good to know where you are at all times in relationship to the reality that is taking place around you.

Here are some reality checks for when you are awake:

- **Always stay consciously aware.** Know how you are interacting with the environment around you. How are people reacting to you? Be careful that you are observing what is true rather than what you may be imaging in your mind's eye. Check your watch, look at your hand, and be aware of what you are experiencing in the moment in your five senses.
- **Be aware of the greater good.** Always be aware of how your actions are affecting others. In NLP, a subject is often asked to imagine into the future to see how the changes they want to make would impact friends and family. Believing that you are doing something to help others often gives you a greater purpose and motivation.
- **Be aware of negative thoughts.** If you constantly have negative thoughts or hear negative voices in your mind's eye, seek professional help to assist you with what you are experiencing. Any lingering thoughts that you may have that go against the laws of society could lead to negative consequences when and if acted upon.
- **Understand the difference between actual psychic information and fantasies.** If you learn to know and trust in the psychic information that naturally comes to you, it can help you be aware of unmanifest realities that you experience and others don't.
- **Be aware of obsessing over something or someone.** If you are obsessed with a particular person, it may be blurring your reality of the situation. You may think someone is madly in love with you who isn't. It is possible you may be getting a past-life feeling or emotion about someone who is not in the same role in this lifetime. What may have been appropriate in another lifetime may not be appropriate in this lifetime. Always remind yourself to stay aware of your emotions. Just because you feel the way you do doesn't mean that another person feels the same way.

Lucid dream fantasies are not a danger unless the fantasy takes over reality in your waking life. If you find that this is the case, look for a professional counselor or clergy to help you sort things out in your mind. When you are aware of your waking reality, you are also ready to experience incredible fantasies in your lucid dreams.

Put Yourself in the Shoes of Someone Else

You can use your psychic abilities in lucid dreams to learn how to help people and animals. What if you could know what was wrong with a person or a pet by experiencing a little of what they are going through? Perhaps you have a natural healing ability that allows you to help the person or the pet to improve their health. In a lucid dream, you can experience what is going on and then change it. You can suggest to yourself that you will continue to send loving healing energy after the lucid dream or lucid dream trance has ended.

FACT

There are a couple of reasons why you would want to put yourself in someone else's shoes. Experiencing what someone else does may well help and inspire you to do better. Also, knowing someone else's mind may help you understand how and why they act the way they do. You may find that you are a good profiler.

Remember that the way you imagine is different from anyone else, and when you intend to have a lucid dream where you can experience how someone like Edgar Cayce connected to the universe, you will do it the way that it is natural for you. What you may gain is the knowledge of how it worked for him so that you can apply this knowledge to how your mind works to reach similar results. Your lucid dream experience may just give you the confidence to develop your psychic gifts.

Be Someone Important

Perhaps you have wanted to experience what it would be like to be someone else. It could be someone famous. They may be alive now or someone that lived during a different time period. You may want to find out what it would be like to be a friend or an adversary in your current life. It may be a musician, an artist, a writer, or an athlete.

So who would you like to be? You may already know or you may want to take a moment and think of whose shoes you would like to step into. Remember that this is a fantasy, so you don't have to have a major reason to have a lucid dream that you are someone or something else. You can choose on the spur of the moment, especially if you are using an altered state of consciousness lucid-dream trance. You can also pick a subject who appears in a random dream when you become consciously aware that you are dreaming.

Fantasy Lucid Dream Exercise

Here is a fantasy lucid dream exercise you can use as part of your intentions for a dream-induced lucid dream, as part of a walking-induced lucid dream technique, for a menmonic-induced lucid dream, or as an induction for a fantasy lucid dream trance. You can set a goal for pure pleasure or for a specific purpose. Once you have decided, create your intentions and remind yourself of them several times a day as you prepare for your lucid dream experience. Remind yourself to be aware of what is taking place around you during your waking time as you repeat your intentions to prime yourself to stay aware while you are sleeping.

- Choose the time that you want to experience a lucid dream or lucid dream trance. At that time make yourself comfortable, take a deep breath, and slowly exhale. Feel gratitude and unconditional love surrounding you and flowing through your heart. With this gratitude in your mind, repeat your lucid dream fantasy intentions. Remind yourself that you will stay consciously aware as you drift into sleep or a lucid dream trance.
- As you continue to slowly breathe in and out, be aware of your muscles relaxing from your head down to the bottoms of your feet. Let yourself feel the excitement and intrigue of the fantasy lucid dream experience that is waiting for you when you become consciously aware that you are dreaming. If you want, you can slowly count down from five to zero, reminding yourself of your fantasy lucid dream intentions between each count. You can feel yourself drifting deeper and deeper into sleep while staying consciously aware.
- If you are familiar with the induction process, you can just let yourself drift off into sleep or an altered state of consciousness trance at a rate that is comfortable for you. Always feel yourself surrounded with love

and gratitude as you drift further and further into sleep or trance. Suggest to yourself that you will be consciously aware when you begin to dream or receive trance dream images in your mind's eye. Suggest to yourself that when you realize that you are dreaming, you will prove it to yourself with a reality test.

- Now that you are consciously aware and know you are experiencing a dream, you are ready to enjoy your lucid dream fantasy. You may experience your dream any way you desire through all of your senses in your mind's eye. If you wake up in a dream, take a moment and recall the images that you were experiencing while you were dreaming and imagine that the dream is continuing. As the dream continues in your mind's eye, let yourself drift back to sleep, staying consciously aware of the dream. Remind yourself that you are now in control of the dream and experience your fantasies any way that you want. You are now ready to begin to explore and experience.

- As your lucid dream is ending or you are ready to come back to consciousness from your lucid dream trance, remind yourself that you will fully recall your lucid dream fantasy experience when you awaken or come back to the surface of your conscious mind. Once you have returned to your normal waking state, write up what you have experienced in your dream journal.

ALERT

You always need to be aware of what is fantasy and what is real. If you are inducing a lucid dream fantasy trance, remind yourself to stay consciously aware as you enter a deep altered state. Just as in a regular lucid dream, remind yourself that you are in a trance and in control of the images in your mind.

You can intend to have a lucid dream fantasy every night or whenever you want or desire to. Lucid dream fantasies may be an excellent way for you to balance the stress of everyday life with the opportunity to fantasize creatively and freely in your lucid dreams.

CHAPTER 21

Create Your Future Through Lucid Dreams

Consider what really speaks to you in your mind's eye regarding your purpose in life. In this final chapter, you will identify the passion you feel when you are involved in something good for others that can help motivate you to set your intentions. You will learn how to work with the laws of attraction and quantum physics to help you manifest a path that helps align your soul purpose with your future, aided by your ability to use lucid dreaming or lucid dream trances. You will also understand the importance of establishing a daily routine of gratitude and positive intentions.

What Is It You Really Want?

What is it that you really want, not only to accomplish in lucid dreaming, but in life as a whole? You have learned that lucid dreaming can be a valuable tool in helping you make positive changes in your life. Lucid dreaming is just that: a tool. It is not a solve-all, cure-all, magic wand.

It is, however, an opportunity for you to examine whatever you want or perhaps need for your lucid dream state. You are in charge of choosing what you want to experience. Once you have had your lucid dream experience, you can continue to recall it in your waking life to help you continue toward your goals. It is also a way for you to work with your team to receive their guidance in achieving your aspirations.

Following are some questions to think about that may help you create your goals for the future and set your intentions to use lucid dreaming as a tool to reach them:

- **If you could do anything you want in life to help others, what would that be?** Remember, there are no ifs, ands, or buts here. There are no restrictions on how you think or dream. So many people say, "If only" or "I would, but . . . . When they interject questions into their daydreams, they are creating a reality based on questions. In your lucid dreams, you are free to experience the future that you daydream about in your mind's eye.
- **What is your passion?** What speaks to you in your heart for doing good? Passion and heart power are very positive mind's-eye images that send out strong energy to attract like energy. Even if there is no current logical route to achieving what you are passionate about, because you are focused on it, you may not have to wait long before something out there in the universe sends back a positive response.
- **Is what you are doing now a part of your passion?** Many people want to completely change their lives and go in search of their passion. That may not be necessary. Part of the neurolinguistic programming (NLP) concept of "model building in the mind" is to look at your goal through what you are currently doing. Perhaps you only need to change a part of your life because what you currently do may help you make your transition to something closer to your passion.

- **Does what you are doing now have the potential to help achieve your passion?** Some people use their vocation to help support their life's work. Financial survival is important and necessary. It is okay to attract prosperity to yourself while helping others.
- **What is keeping you from reaching your goals?** Are you stopping yourself or are there others holding you back? What is the reason that something seems out of your control, such as cost or physical limitations? Are there resistances blocking you, such as the fear of taking the risk of succeeding? Give all of these and any other questions you have a chance to speak so that you can get to know what is holding you back from reaching your goals.
- **What is the first step you can take now toward reaching your goals?** People often do not try to reach for their passions because it seems impossible to get there. The path is filled with uncertainties and improbabilities. There are no boundaries when it comes to experiences in your lucid dreams. You have already taken your first steps forward by answering these questions. Now it's time to consider your next step. It's time to take your goals from dreams to realities.

ALERT

Many people don't intend that they can be mentally, physically, spiritually, and emotionally taken care of. They often struggle as they strive to help others. If you are one of those people, you might consider trusting and believing that if you are doing it right, then your team will amply provide for you.

You may want to take some time as you ponder these questions and make some notes in your dream journal. Even if you are not convinced that lucid dreaming works well for you, this process can help you define your life goals. Remember that you can use the information you gather to help you set intentions for lucid dreaming and altered-state dream trances as well as for prayer or any other type of communication with the universe or your guides.

Clearly Set Your Intentions

Did you learn anything about your passions for doing good and helping others when you considered the questions in the last section? If you already understood them, that's wonderful—if you were able to get some insight about yourself and what is blocking you from reaching your goals. The more you give yourself permission to trust and believe that you have a purpose, the more this thought will stay in your conscious mind. Life often has a way of distracting us from honoring what we feel in our hearts. It is never too late to make positive changes in your life.

Once you have identified what that missing piece or passion is, you can begin to investigate how you can get in sync with your purpose. Lucid dreaming is a great mechanism to check out a variety of potential future routes that you can take as you move toward honoring your passions. In fact, you can use lucid dreaming techniques all along the path of your life's purpose.

Here are some suggestions to help you clearly set your intentions to create your future:

- **Define your long-range goals.** Where would you imagine yourself in five years if there were no obstacles in your path? This is a long-range goal. You may already know what that is or you may be looking for the answer. For some people it is hard to see what life will be like tomorrow, to say nothing about five years out. Don't worry about what kind of answers you come up with as long as your intentions are for the greater good. Your long-range goal at the moment may seem like a dream or a wish.
- **Think of a five-year plan for reaching your long-range goals.** What could you imagine accomplishing in the first year? Take a moment and create a dream timeline for each of the years leading to your goal completion. Remember this timeline is only a concept that can be adapted and changed as you move toward accomplishing your goals.
- **Consider the resistances that could stop you from reaching your goals.** Whatever they are, it is important to resolve or find a way around them for you to stay on course. Take a moment and consider a resistance. Is it caused by you or someone else? If it is by someone else, why are they standing in the way? What can be done to work out the issues?

When you are planning for the future, it is always important to know the realties of the present. Looking at obstacles or resistances as opportunities rather than roadblocks may help change your outlook toward accomplishing your goals. The goal, after all, is to work toward achieving your goals with gratitude and joy, not as if you were fighting a battle to succeed.

Verify Your Passion

Perhaps the next step on your journey is to intend to experience a lucid dream or lucid dream trance that helps you verify what your passion for life is. Create a lucid dream intention to investigate what it would be like to be living your passion. You can play out several scenarios, including working out the resistances that are currently holding you back. You can work with your faith or guides to help you play out your dream. Suggest to yourself that you will fully recall your lucid dreams after you come back to full wakefulness.

You can use lucid dream techniques every step of the way on your journey through life as you seek to honor the passion that is in your soul. It is good to have flexibility built into your intentions as you work to achieve your goals. One suggestion is that when you write down and say your intentions to yourself several times a day, you include a phrase that goes something like: "I am grateful that I am being guided to reach my goals or something better."

The Laws of Attraction and Quantum Physics

Let's go back to the Laws of Attraction one more time. Take a moment and think about the words you have been saying to others and to yourself in your mind. Have you been using words like "if," "but," "can't," "never," or "won't"? The instant negative words pop into your mind they begin defeating you from reaching your goals. They can become roadblocks along your path of life.

How many times have you said to yourself, "I wish I could have?" Do you remember the children's book *The Little Engine That Could*? The gist of the story is that there was a train of railroad cars that needed to be pulled on the track over a mountain. All the big engines tried and failed, and it came down to the littlest one. Of course, no one thought the little engine could handle the load.

When the little engine began to pull, it chanted to itself, "I think I can," over and over. It slowly inched its way up the mountain until it got to the top. As it started down the other side the chant changed to, "I knew I could." The message in the story is move forward one inch at a time doing the best you think you can, and you may be surprised where you end up along your life's path. Positive thoughts can bring about positive results.

Matter Is Energy

On a single-cell level, all matter is composed of energy. Each cell is an entity unto itself and is attracted to other energy or matter that puts out compatible energy. Like attracts like while negative energy attracts negativity. Thoughts are a form of invisible matter with energy that attracts a physical action in harmony with the original thoughts. The way you think helps create what you attract back to yourself.

QUESTION

What is quantum physics?
Max Planck determined in the early 1900s through the study of microscopic matter and energy that the same laws of science apply to macroscopic matter, which is large enough to be seen with your naked eyes. Microscopic energy is free to travel long distances, while visual mass cannot.

If a part of you really wants to achieve or attract something and another part doubts that this will happen, you are sending out conflicting thoughts that block your ability to attract positive results. In order to work with the Law of Attraction, it is important to create intentions that do not conflict with any energy that you may send into the universe in thought form. In other words, it means that you need to intend what you believe in. If you hope to get a new job but really don't believe you will be able to get one, chances are that you will not get it.

Faith and Belief and Energy

You know that one of the steps toward successful lucid dreaming is to create intentions that stay in your conscious mind. You do this by reminding yourself over and over again during the day about what you intend to experience in a lucid dream. The same is true of intending a lucid dream to help you connect with your life purpose. It is your faith that this is right and good for you that sends out positive energy to attract back positive results.

Belief is an important part of the equation for attracting positive results. When you have confidence that something out there is looking out for you, you are united with yourself and your team in sending out positive energy. Because energy is free to travel, it will find and attract compatible energy, which in turn manifests in either thought actions or mass. For instance, the thought of wanting a different car is creating the reality of the car in your mind, and the Law of Attraction, as defined in quantum physics, are set in motion. A lucid dream where you already own the car can help reinforce the energy you sent out related to the Law of Attracting the car.

Take a moment and consider how you can intend to experience a lucid dream that will help produce positive energy for attracting a positive direction in your life in tune with your passion and purpose. Once you have defined your intentions, repeat them to yourself several times a day. Do the same before you drift off to sleep or prepare to enter a lucid dream trance.

The Power of Your Heart

Now you are back to heart power again. Gratitude is another big part of the laws of attraction. That starts with unconditional love. Unconditional love is a love that doesn't come with expectations. If you have a memory of unconditional love, take a moment and experience it in your mind's eye. That feeling, coupled with gratitude, translates into thought energy.

Remember the fact that the heart puts out sixty times the energy as the brain. Add that powerful energy to your intention energy with the belief that like attracts like, and you are creating in sync with the Law of Attraction. Add your faith that what you are intending is already a reality, and let yourself experience this in your mind's eye. You may see it, hear it, feel it, taste it, smell it, or just know it. Remember to accept that what you have intended is real, and thank the universe or whatever you believe in for manifesting it.

Positive Energy

When you have developed the habit of starting your day with gratitude and connecting to unconditional love, you are starting out with a thought reality that is powered by your heart. The reality of love attracts positive reactions to your heart's energy. The more you continue to find moments during the day to pause in your mind's eye, take a breath, and feel gratitude and unconditional love in your heart, no matter what is taking place around you, the more you continually send out positive energy. Your positive energy alone can have an incredible effect on the conditions you are experiencing at that time or in the near future. Your mind's eye and heart actions may possibly make a difference in how your day and the day of others around you is going.

ESSENTIAL

When you add your short- and long-range goals to your intentions of gratitude and love, you are defining and directing your heart energy to specific targets. The trick here is to have gratitude that your specific goals are already achieved or real, even if you do not know how they will be proven to you.

All this, of course, relates back to quantum physics and the belief that thoughts are energy and energy is not stuck within a mass. So your thoughts are free to travel outside of yourself to your specific goals that you have intended. Your mind's-eye actions then follow the laws of attraction that your intentions, magnified by your heart energy, will attract positive results.

Change Your Wording

For those worries and anxious thoughts you may have been sending out that have been attracting more worry and anxiety back, take a moment and think of how you can change the language in your mind's eye to gratitude and love. Pay attention to the words you have been uttering out loud to yourself or to others and the word thoughts that you are creating in your mind. Are they negative or positive? Now consider for a moment what these words and thoughts have been attracting back to you.

You may want to make some notes in your dream journal on the language you have been using on yourself and others. You can set intentions to examine any negative thoughts you have been creating from the nonordinary state of a lucid dream or lucid dream trance. Focus on one of those thoughts during the day and become aware of when it enters your mind. Intend that you will be able to use a lucid dream or trance to investigate why and how the negative thoughts originated in your mind. Use the lucid dream or trance technique that works best for you and investigate how to change your mind's language.

Traveling with Help from the Other Side

Another important piece in creating your future is your belief. If you are feeling lost in life or out of sync with what really satisfies you in your heart, then you know that there is something not right in your life. That something may be just part of honoring what is your passion or something that creates a feeling of unconditional love in your heart. For many people this is where they want to be in life but either don't know how to achieve it or feel they are being held back from reaching it. Have you ever had this feeling of being stuck with no way to move forward?

If you are one of those who feel this way, perhaps you can take a moment to examine why you feel the way you do. The key is to know in your heart. Once you acknowledge what you know, it is the willingness to trust and believe that your knowing is right. When you add your belief that you are not alone and have something that travels with you, you can change the thoughts you are creating in your mind from negative to positive. How you define what is helping you is your choice—as long as it is a force for the good.

Maximize Your Heart Power

If you believe that there is something with you, whether you know exactly what it is or not, you can use what you believe to help you create powerful mind's-eye imagery connecting your belief with your purpose. When you create your goals with the knowledge that something is working with you, and thank that something with gratitude and love from your heart, you are maximizing your heart power. Even if you are unsure of how you want your life to go from where you are at the moment, all you need to intend is that it goes in the direction your team and belief are guiding it toward.

ALERT

Sometimes it's hard to learn to trust that there really is something out there in the universe that is always available to guide you on your journey. Perhaps you might look back over your life when miracles have happened in the past. You just may find proof that there has been something with you all along.

This little saying helps shift the burden of the weight of success from your shoulders to your team: "If I am doing it right, then all I have to do is take my small steps and trust and believe that my team is putting it all together." When you have a thought or feeling that is a knowing, it may be your team nudging you to take a step of faith to bring your knowing to complete reality.

Dealing with Fear

It can be scary to act on knowing alone. It is okay to feel fear. Without knowing or trusting in something that is with you, fear can completely take over and sabotage your heart's ability to send out positive energy. When you encounter fear, examine what you are afraid of in your mind's eye and turn your fear over to your team to help overcome it. Just knowing that your team is there can help you take the next step toward positive success.

Your lucid dreams can also help you connect with your team in nonordinary realities. Within your dream or lucid dream trance state, you can experience the guidance your team provides you as you progress toward what you know in your heart to be true. You can then use your lucid dream experiences to reinforce your positive energy as you attract to you the best route to your life's purpose.

Manifesting Positive Results

Now it's time to consider the results of all your positive work, the manifestation of your intentions. As you remember, there are two types of reality: manifest and unmanifest. The manifest reality is everything that has a physical mass that can be seen with your naked eyes. It is something that is provable to the standards of what society considers being real. The unmanifest is just as real but is not known to most people, nor can it be proved at the current time to be real.

Unmanifest reality is energy. As you have already learned, according to quantum physics, microscopic mass is energy that is free to move differently than macroscopic or larger mass. It can travel long distances in search of like energy or the intention one is sending out of her heart. Do you feel like you have gone around in a circle? You have.

The Formula

So what is the formula for manifesting your future? Perhaps it is something like:

Passion and Knowing

+ Goals

+ Clear Intentions

+ Belief

+ Gratitude and Unconditional Love

+ Heart Energy

+ The Law of Attraction

= MANIFESTED RESULTS

Add to that your ability to experience lucid dreams or lucid dream trances, and you are attracting like, which produces positive results; the results that you have experienced in your lucid dreams or lucid dream trances.

FACT

You have many different options and reasons for manifesting incredible improvements in your life through lucid dreaming and lucid dream trances. You can manifest abundance in physical, mental, spiritual, and emotional aspects of your life with the belief that these manifestations are helping you honor your life's purpose.

When needed or desired, you can also create lucid dream trance imagery in a moment by taking a breath and connecting to your team. In that moment, your heart is sending out your intentions with gratitude, love, and the acceptance that your team is right there with you, manifesting a positive solution for your intention.

Get into a Routine of Using Lucid Dreams

So now you know some of the secrets of successful people who knowingly or naturally use their lucid dream and lucid dream altered state trance abilities to continuously attract and manifest success in their lives. You have this same ability. Remember that your route is going to be a little different than anyone else's. The route is not the main concern; it is the destination. In the Law of Attraction, it is not worrying about how your intention will manifest itself; it is the belief that it will.

The more you can experience these intentions in your mind's eye through your five senses, the stronger your energy becomes as it is projected out to your intended goals or targets. This brings you back to the fact that during lucid dreams or lucid dream trances, you have the freedom of nonreality to explore your intended goals from nonordinary vantage points without the restrictions (the buts and ifs) that exist in your conscious mind. Once you have had these experiences, you can bring the information gathered back to your conscious waking mind. The result is that you can now recall your lucid dream experiences to help create even more focused images in your mind's eye that can help narrow down how and where you may choose to project your intentions, using your heart energy.

Gratitude

There is probably no greater goal or desire than the feeling that your life is serving a purpose. It is a wonderful feeling to have joy and unconditional love in your heart, even in normal life situations where it is hard to find. The path to joy is gratitude. Start by being consciously aware every day of something you are grateful for. Establish a gratitude routine.

Teamwork

Also establish the habit of creating positive intentions every day that include working with your team. When you have a worry, thank your team with gratitude for finding the right solution. In your daily routine of creating and repeating your intentions, suggest to yourself that your team will guide you in your lucid dreams or dream trance states to experience the best positive results.

Imagination

It is not necessary that you lucid dream every night on a regular basis to benefit from establishing a daily routine of creating positive intentions. If you get into the habit of using the imagery in your mind's eye during even a light altered state of consciousness, you can imagine a lucid dream that relates to your intentions. This action in itself will help spawn regular lucid dreams.

ESSENTIAL

Where do your thoughts come from? Do you generate them in your ego mind or are they from an outside source that has given you a thought to imagine? Perhaps this is a good lucid dream project for you. You can intend to have a lucid dream to find the source behind your thoughts.

You have learned that lucid dreaming can be a powerful tool to help you journey through your life. Lucid dreaming is not an end-all by itself. In fact, it is really just a beginning; it is a mechanism that can help you make major positive changes in your life. Now it is up to you, if you choose, to give yourself permission to take the risk of succeeding. Dream on.

APPENDIX A

Glossary of Terms

Akashic Records

An imaginary book believed to hold every deed, word, feeling, thought, and intent of every soul in the universe

Astral projection

Traveling in your mind to a spiritual world

Breath work

A breathing exercise that helps the participant gain spiritual insights

Channel

A conduit for something to pass through. A psychic channel is a person who has another spirit or entity communicate through them.

Clear light of the void

Mystical state of being

Conscious dreaming

A dream experience in which the participant is consciously aware that he is dreaming

Conscious mind

The surface of the mind; the communication center where you process thoughts and ideas

Cosmos

The cosmos pertains to the systematic order of the universe.

DILD

Dream-induced lucid dream

Dowsing

A method of finding water or objects using psychic tools

Dream

Sensory images experienced while a person is asleep

Fantasy

Images in the mind created by imagination that are not provable in ordinary realities

Flooding technique

The use of several sensory stimulants at once to confuse the conscious mind and allow a suggestion to be given to the unconscious mind

Future pacing

A term in hypnosis used to deepen your altered state of consciousness by a suggestion anticipating a positive response

Guided imagery

The process of inducing a trance or altered state of consciousness

Hologram

An image that changes when viewed from a different angle

Hypnagogic state

Transition between wakefulness and sleep, also spelled hypnogogic

Hypnosis

An altered state of consciousness in which the unconscious mind accepts suggestions

Law of Attraction

The concept that you bring into your life what you send out

Lucid

Being consciously aware of one's thoughts

Lucid dream

Being aware while you are in a dream

Lucid living

A unique way of looking at and experiencing life from a somewhat-detached state of consciousness while at the same time being fully aware of both the real and spiritual worlds

Manifest reality

Everything that can be touched, seen, heard, smelled, or tasted

Mantra

A word or a phrase repeated over and over to help raise the spiritual vibrational level of the participant

Medium

A person through whom the deceased can communicate with the living

MILD

Mnemonic-induced lucid dreams

Mind's eye

Images created in the mind through the five senses of seeing, hearing, feeling, tasting, and smelling

Muscle memory

A physical action remembered by the unconscious mind

Near-death experience

A form of out-of-body experience

Nightmare

A dream that causes the dreamer to experience fear

NLP

Neurolinguistic programming. A communication technique developed by Grinder and Bandler to change and improve thinking processes

Oneirology

The scientific study of dreams

Oneness

The feeling or belief that everything is connected through the core of the universe, also thought of as God

Other Side

The world of spirits and the dead that exists on another plane of reality than the normal world

Out-of-body experience

When energy leaves your body and goes someplace else

Paradigm

A thought pattern

Pendulum

A tool for dowsing that consists of a string or chain with a weight at the end

Posthypnotic suggestion

A suggestion given during a hypnosis trance that continues after the trance is over

Power of suggestion

A suggestion that others accept as real without actual proof

Psychic

The ability to obtain information from sources that have no scientifically proven basis, such as intuition or the supernatural

Quantum physics

The concept of physics that maintains that microscopic mass has different rules of movement than macroscopic mass

Reality

Something that can be proven to exist

Reframe

The installation of a new habit into the unconscious mind

Regression

To go back to an earlier point in time

REM

Rapid eye movement; it is most intense in the latter stage of a dream.

Remote viewing

Looking at a scene while traveling there in your mind

Self-hypnosis

The process of inducing a trance state in yourself

Scrying

A visual aid, such as looking into a crystal ball, used to gather psychic information, especially relating to the future

Shaman

A healer; also called medicine man, witch doctor, mystic, sorcerer, diviner, etc.

Theosophy

Knowledge that comes through spiritual, not intellectual, means

Tunnel vision

Extremely narrow viewpoint

Unconscious mind

The storage area of the mind that contains all your past experiences; also referred to as the subconscious

Underworld

In shamanism, a place below the earth's surface where power animals are believed to exist and where humans came from and return to after death

Unmanifest reality

Something real that cannot be seen, touched, or readily explained

WILD

Wake-induced lucid dream

Zone

A form of trance where time and distance become distorted

APPENDIX B

Additional Resources

Further Reading

Bro, Harmon H. *Edgar Cayce on Dreams.* (New York: Warner Books, 1968).

Byrne, Rhonda. *The Secret.* (New York: Atria Books, 2006).

Cheung, Theresa. *The Element Encyclopedia of 20,000 Dreams.* (London: Harper Element, 2006).

Dyer, Wayne W. *The Shift: Taking Your Life from Ambition to Meaning.* (Carlsbad, CA: Hay House, Inc., 2010).

Evans-Wentz, W. Y. *Tibetan Yoga and Secret Doctrines: Seven Books of Wisdom of the Great Path, According to the Late Lama Kazi Dawa-Samdup's English Rendering.* (London: Oxford University Press, 1935).

Freud, Sigmund. *Interpretations of Dreams.* (New York: Avon Books, 1965).

Gallop, D., editor. *Aristotle: On Sleep and Dreams (Classical Texts).* (Great Britain: Aris & Phillips, 1996).

Godwin, Malcolm. *The Lucid Dreamer: A Waking Guide for the Traveler Between Worlds.* (New York: Simon & Schuster, 1994).

Green, Celia. *Lucid Dreaming.* (London: Hamish Hamilton, 1968).

Green, Celia and Charles McCreery. *Apparitions.* (London: Hamish Hamilton, 1975).

Green, Celia and Charles McCreery. *Lucid Dreaming: The Paradox of Consciousness During Sleep.* (New York: Routledge, 1994).

Grof, Stanislav. *The Holotropic Mind: The Three Levels of Human Consciousness and How They Shape Our Lives.* (San Francisco: HarperCollins, 1992).

Haley, Jay. *Uncommon Therapy: The Psychiatric Techniques of Milton H. Erickson, M.D.* (New York: W. W. Norton & Company, 1993).

Harner, Michael. *The Way of the Shaman.* (San Francisco: HarperOne, 1990).

Hathaway, Michael R. *The Complete Idiot's Guide to Discovering Your Past Lives, 2nd Edition.* (New York: Alpha Books, Penguin Group, 2011).

Hathaway, Michael R. *The Everything® Hypnosis Book.* (Avon, MA: Adams Media Corporation, 2003).

Hathaway, Michael R. *The Everything® Psychic Book, 2nd Edition.* (Avon, MA: Adams Media Corporation, 2011).

Hathaway, Michael R. *It's Time to Simplify Your Soul's Code: The Back-to-Basics Spirituality Book.* (West Conshohocken, PA: Infinity Publishing, 2007).

Holzer, Hans. *Fate Presents . . . the Psychic Side of Dreams.* (St. Paul, MN: Llewellyn Publications, 1994).

Huxley, Aldous. *Doors of Perception.* (New York: HarperCollins/Perennial Library, 1970).

LaBerge, Stephen. *Lucid Dreaming: The Power of Being Aware and Awake in Your Dreams.* (New York: Ballantine Books, 1998).

LaBerge, Stephen and Howard Rheingold. *Exploring the World of Lucid Dreaming.* (New York: Ballantine Books, 1991).

Larsen, Stephen. *The Shaman's Doorway: Opening Imagination to Power and Myth.* (Rochester, VT: Inner Traditions, 1998).

Lohff, David C. *The Dream Directory: The Comprehensive Guide to Analysis and Interpretation, With Explanations for More than 350 Symbols and Theories.* (Philadelphia: Courage Books, 1998).

Moody, Raymond A. Jr. *Life After Life: The Investigation of a Phenomenon—Survival of Bodily Death.* (New York: HarperCollins, 2001).

Moss, C. Scott. *Hypnotic Investigation of Dreams.* (New York: John Wiley & Sons, 1967).

Moss, Robert. *Conscious Dreaming: A Spiritual Path for Everyday Life.* (New York: Three Rivers Press, 1996).

O'Connor, Cathleen. *The Everything Law of Attraction Dream Dictionary: An A to Z Guide to Using Your Dreams to Attract Success, Prosperity, and Love.* (Avon, MA: Adams Media, 2010).

Rinpoche, Tenzin Wangyal. *The Tibetan Yogas of Dream and Sleep.* (Ithaca, NY: Snow Lion Publications,1998).

Rosen, Sidney, editor. *My Voice Will Go With You: The Teaching Tales of Milton H. Erickson.* (New York: W. W. Norton & Company, 1982).

Sugrue, Thomas. *There Is a River: The Story of Edgar Cayce.* (New York: Holt, Rinehart and Winston, 1942).

Thurston, Mark A. *How to Interpret Your Dreams: Practical Techniques Based on the Edgar Cayce Approach.* (Virginia Beach, VA: A.R.E. Press, 1978).

Urantia Foundation Editors. *The Urantia Book: Revealing the Mysteries of God, the Universe, Jesus, and Ourselves.* (Chicago: Urantia Foundation, 1955).

Watts, Alan W. *The Joyous Cosmology: Adventures in the Chemistry of Consciousness.* (New York: Vintage Books, 1965).

Websites

Association for Research and Enlightenment
Holistic Health, Spiritual Growth, Education, and home of the Edgar Cayce Foundation
www.edgarcayce.org

Crystalinks
Metaphysics and Science Website
www.crystalinks.com

Global Oneness
Transforming the planet through an increase in spiritual awareness
www.experiencefestival.com

Celia Green
Research on lucid dreams
www.celiagreen.com

Dr. Lisa Halpin
Originator of HypnoCoaching®
www.hypnocoachcertification.com

Michael R. Hathaway
Author of this book
www.michaelhathaway.com
www.whitemountainhypnosiscenter.com
www.messagefromthemountain.podcastpeople.com

The Lucidity Institute, Inc.

Lucid dreaming, consciousness, and dream yoga with Stephen LaBerge

www.lucidity.com

The Matrix

The Remote Viewers Newsletter

www.trvnews.com

The Milton H. Erickson Foundation

Dedicated to promoting and advancing the contributions made by the late Milton H. Erickson to the health sciences

www.erickson-foundation.org

National Guild of Hypnotists

Hypnosis

www.ngh.net

Science Magazine

Article by Eugene Aserinsky and Nathaniel Kleitman. *Regularly Occurring Periods of Eye Motility and Concomitant Phenomena, During Sleep.*

www.sciencemag.org

Shaman Links

Educational resources on the subject of shamanism

www.shamanlinks.net

Society for Shamanic Practitioners

Committed to the re-emergence of shamanic practices that promote healthy individuals and viable communities

www.shamansociety.org

The Theosophical Society in America

Organization that promotes willingness in its members to examine any concept and believe with an open mind and respect for others
www.theosophical.org

The Urantia Book Fellowship

Cultivating the spirit of religion
www.urantiabook.org

The Urantia Book Historical Society

Fostering an awareness and appreciation of the Urantia Book through its heritage, origins, background, development, and general history
www.ubhistory.org

What the Bleep Do We Know

A movie where science and spirituality come together
www.whatthebleep.com

Dream Journal

Use these pages to start your lucid dream journal.

DREAM JOURNAL

Index

Guides
help from, 130–31
mysticism and, 223–24
psychic abilities and,
229–31

Hallucinations, 19, 22, 75,
214, 238
Healing abilities, 233–36
Healing exercises, 185–86
Healing others, 184–86
Healing past experiences,
233–34
Healing process, 183–87
Healing rituals, 16
Health, improving, 175–87
dreams of, 177–78, 183–84,
241
exercises for, 181–83,
185–86
healing others, 184–86
image of, 178–81
Hearing images, 89
Heart power, 59, 94–95, 126–
29, 133, 253–56
Helping others, 184–86,
244–45
Hologram, 153, 263
Holotropic Breathwork, 21
Huxley, Aldous, 20
Hypnagogic state, 33, 53–54,
63–66, 95–97, 105–6, 263
Hypnosis. *See also* Self-
hypnosis
definition of, 263
explanation of, xi–xii, 3–5,
36

flooding technique, 55
future pacing, 65
hallucinations and, 22
lucid dreams and, 32–36
OBEs and, 77–78
power of suggestion and,
68
visual aids for, 116–17
*The Hypnotic Investigation of
Dreams*, xi–xii
Hypnotic sleep, 16

Image exercises, 94–97,
120–22
Imagery, guided, 111, 121–22,
197, 263
Images, and senses, 87–94.
See also Mind images
Imagination, 259–60
Intention exercise, 59–60,
106–7
Interactive facilitated lucid
dreams, 36–37
Interpretations of Dreams, 18

Job skills, 158–59
Journaling, 26–27, 210–12,
277–81
Joyous Cosmology, 20

Kleitman, Nathaniel, 10

LaBerge, Stephen, xi–xii, 13,
23–24, 29, 31–32, 55, 101, 116

Language, changing, 254–55
Law of Attraction
definition of, 31, 264
faith and, 195, 222
mantra and, 52
quantum physics and, 251–58
recalling dreams and, 160
Leary, Timothy, 20
Life After Life, 78
Life magazine, 20
Lohff, David, 9
Loved ones, contacting,
228–29
Loved ones, visiting, 208–10
Lucid, definition of, 264
Lucid dreaming. *See also*
Lucid dreams
benefits of, 5–7
concerns about, 7–9
deep dreaming, 4–5
explanation of, 2–3
history of, 13–24
power mind images for,
85–97
on purpose, 11–12
reasons for, x
techniques for, 25–37
tools for, 111–22
*Lucid Dreaming: The
Paradox of Consciousness
During Sleep*, 22
*Lucid Dreaming: The Power
of Being Aware and Awake
in Your Dreams*, 24
Lucid dreams. *See also* Lucid
dreaming
awareness of, 43–46,
100–106

We Have

EVERYTHING®

on Anything!

With more than 19 million copies sold, the Everything® series has become one of America's favorite resources for solving problems, learning new skills, and organizing lives. Our brand is not only recognizable—it's also welcomed.

The series is a hand-in-hand partner for people who are ready to tackle new subjects—like you!

For more information on the Everything® series, please visit www.adamsmedia.com

The Everything® list spans a wide range of subjects, with more than 500 titles covering 25 different categories:

Business	History	Reference
Careers	Home Improvement	Religion
Children's Storybooks	Everything Kids	Self-Help
Computers	Languages	Sports & Fitness
Cooking	Music	Travel
Crafts and Hobbies	New Age	Wedding
Education/Schools	Parenting	Writing
Games and Puzzles	Personal Finance	
Health	Pets	

CD Credits

Embryonic Breathing [0:01:48]
Gongs by Daniel Cantor ©2010

Five Minute Mid-Day Refresh [0:04:48]
Magic Gong from Freesound by Gezortenplotz

The Still, Small Voice (based on 1 Kings 19:11–13) [0:02:00]
Flute played By Nathan Berla-Shulock ©2010

The Three Assignments [0:01:33]
Waves on Beach from Freesound by Acclivity

A Sikh Meditation [0:01:10]
Pensive Vibes 6&7 by Daniel Cantor ©2010

A Prayer for Lovingkindness [0:02:17]
Birds from Freesound by Crk365

Peace Meditation [0:00:50]
Tibetan Chant from Freesound by DJ Griffin